Teaching Law by Design for Adjuncts

Teaching Law by Design for Adjuncts

Sophie Sparrow

PROFESSOR, UNIVERSITY OF NEW HAMPSHIRE SCHOOL OF LAW,
FORMERLY FRANKLIN PIERCE LAW CENTER
CONSULTANT, INSTITUTE FOR LAW TEACHING AND LEARNING

Gerald Hess

PROFESSOR, GONZAGA UNIVERSITY SCHOOL OF LAW,
CO-DIRECTOR, INSTITUTE FOR LAW
TEACHING AND LEARNING

Michael Hunter Schwartz

PROFESSOR, WASHBURN UNIVERSITY SCHOOL OF LAW,
CO-DIRECTOR, INSTITUTE FOR LAW
TEACHING AND LEARNING

CAROLINA ACADEMIC PRESS
Durham, North Carolina

Library of Congress Cataloging-in-Publication Data

Sparrow, Sophie.
  Teaching law by design for adjuncts / Sophie Sparrow, Gerald F.
Hess, Michael Hunter Schwartz .
    p. cm.
  Includes bibliographical references.
  ISBN 978-1-59460-869-8 (alk. paper)
  1. Law--Study and teaching. 2. Law teachers--Vocational guid-
ance. I. Hess, Gerald F., 1952- II. Schwartz, Michael Hunter. III.
Title.

  K100.S68 2010
  340.071'1--dc22

                  2010016785

          CAROLINA ACADEMIC PRESS
                700 Kent Street
          Durham, North Carolina 27701
            Telephone (919) 489-7486
               Fax (919) 493-5668
               www.cap-press.com

        Printed in the United States of America
                  2015 Printing

This book is dedicated to

My parents, Lydia and Edward, who inspired me to never stop learning.
— Sophie

Adjunct professors, who have so much to offer our students.
— Gerry

My daughter, Kendra Leigh Schwartz, as a thank you for her steadfast and sometimes daunting belief that excellence in teaching is the only acceptable standard, for the joy and pride being her father brings me, and for her ability to make me laugh many times every day.
— Mike

Contents

Introduction

Our primary goal in this book is to provide concrete suggestions for adjunct professors about how to design and conduct all aspects of teaching law students, from sequencing a course to grading an exam. New and experienced adjuncts can apply the book's principles to any law school class.

We hope the book helps you and your students enjoy teaching and learning in law school. At the same time, we caution you not to feel compelled to adopt every suggestion in this book. Not only has none of us adopted every suggestion in this book, but we doubt anyone could do so. Instead, make small rather than wholesale changes, evaluate the effectiveness of every new practice you try, keep doing the things that work, discard the things that don't work, and, above all, aspire to continuous improvement.

The first chapter provides a legal education-focused overview of the research on teaching and learning. The second chapter captures the student perspective on law teaching and learning. Chapters 3 through 7 focus on fundamental elements of teaching: course design, class design, motivation, teaching methods, and assessment. Chapter 8 focuses on things law teachers can do to systematically improve themselves as teachers. Chapter 9 contains a list of teaching and learning resources, including books, articles, videos, and websites.

We hope that this book will be a valuable resource for adjunct professors. We recommend three other important recourses to help adjuncts excel as teachers.

The first resource is the Appendix for this book and for *Teaching Law by Design: Engaging Students from the Syllabus to the Final*

Exam (a more detailed version of this book). The Appendix has many examples of syllabi, exercises, handouts, grading rubrics, and other documents related to Chapters 3–8. The Appendix is available for free on the website of the Institute for Law Teaching and Learning at http://lawteaching.org/resources/books/teachinglawby design/teachinglawbydesign-appendices.pdf.

The second resource is the American Bar Association's *Adjunct Faculty Handbook* (2005). This 47-page document contains helpful advice on preparing to teach, conducting the class, grading, and working with your law school. The *Handbook* is free and available on the ABA's website at http://www.abanet.org/legaled/publications/ adjuncthandbook/adjuncthandbook.pdf.

Finally, the associate dean at your law school is a critical resource. The associate dean will be familiar with your law school's policies, resources, programs, and culture. It is important for you to know your school's policies and rules before you begin teaching. We encourage you to develop a strong working relationship with your associate dean. Understanding your associate dean's expectations will help you avoid common problems the associate dean may have encountered in the past. If the associate dean is unable to address your questions directly, she may provide you with a list of other faculty you can use as a resource. As part of our research for this book, we asked associate deans for their advice for adjunct professors. Four themes emerged in their advice: (1) be prepared to work hard — many adjuncts underestimate the difficulty of teaching a law school course; (2) develop objectives for your courses and class sessions; (3) establish and maintain a respectful, challenging classroom environment; and (4) comply with the school's grading policies and deadlines. We agree with this advice and believe that this book will help you meet and exceed the expectations of your associate dean.

While we wrote this book in an effort to share what we believe to be core principles of teaching and learning, the book also is sort of a white paper for the "Context and Practice Casebook" series from Carolina Academic Press. The series is designed to apply the principles from this book, as well as other insights and recommendations from Best Practices In Legal Education (CLEA 2007) and Educating Lawyers (Jossey-Bass 2007), to the creation of law school course materials.

We wish to thank the many people who made this book possible. We appreciate the support of our law schools, our students, our families, and the helpful folks at Carolina Academic Press.

Sophie Sparrow
University of New Hampshire School of Law,
formerly Franklin Pierce Law Center
Consultant, Institute for Law Teaching and Learning

Gerald Hess
Gonzaga University School of Law
Co-director, Institute for Law Teaching and Learning

Michael Hunter Schwartz
Washburn University School of Law
Co-director, Institute for Law Teaching and Learning

Teaching Law by Design
for Adjuncts

Chapter 1

What It Means to Be a Teacher

This chapter explores what we know about effective learning and effective teaching.

What We Know about Effective Learning

We have chosen to start a book on teaching with what we know about effective learning. That choice is deliberate. Teaching is effective *only* if it produces significant learning. Significant learning, whether labeled "mastery" or "competency," is the ability to use what one has learned. Thus, law students have learned something significant when they can use their legal skills and knowledge to solve a legal problem.

Cognitive Learning Theory

According to "cognitive theory," students cannot apply skills and knowledge unless they have stored what they learned in an organized, meaningful and useable way. The processes of storing new learning and retrieving stored learning occur according to the sequence depicted below in Illustration 1-1. Although the sequence may appear linear, moving from one place to the next, the process probably is more circular and interactive. Although we describe this "cognitive processing" as a model or theory, there is considerable research supporting its accuracy.

Illustration 1-1. A Model of Cognitive Processing

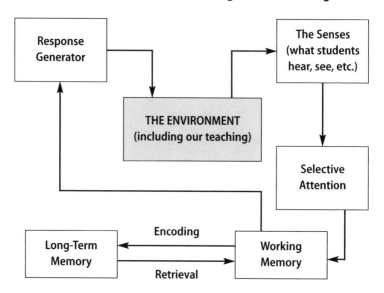

Hundreds of pieces of information reach our students' senses every moment. Humans can attend, however, to only a few of these pieces of information so our students must decide: which stimuli warrant attention? The process of choosing a focus is known as "selective attention." Thus, the learning process is over at the spigot if our students decide to pay attention to their e-mail or their eBay purchases. Of course, all we hear is, "What was the question?"

If our students do pay attention, what we teach passes into their working memory. Students' working memory can retain only a small amount of learning and only for a limited time, but, when our students do something *active* to store their learning in a meaningful way, the information becomes a part of their long-term memory.

For this reason, engaging students in active learning activities is crucial to learning. Active learning activities are those in which students cannot simply sit and listen but must do something to mentally process the concepts we want them to learn. If students are writing about the concepts, discussing them with a peer, figuring out how they relate to each other and to what they already know, students are engaged in active learning. Moreover, the more deeply students think about what they are learning, the more likely they are to remember and use it.

But storing learned skills and knowledge isn't enough. To analyze a problem, students must recall ("retrieve") what they have learned and use that learning to interact with the environment in some way.

Constructivist Learning Theory

Consequently, constructivist theory focuses on the process required for new learning to become a more-or-less permanent part of who the students are. Three crucial learning principles derive from constructivist research. First, learning is a matter of constructing an interpretation from an experience. When students engage with materials in an active, effortful way and reflect on the process, they develop personal understandings. And those personal understandings, having been entirely generated within the student's mind, stay with the student. Thus, significant law student learning only can happen if the law professor provides the students with opportunities to develop such interpretations, to figure things out for themselves.

Constructivists also emphasize the importance of real-world experiences, both in learning activities and assessment. Students learn when their opportunities to construct understandings are authentic, such as when their learning is anchored in a realistic context. Thus, law professors who teach cases and rules in the context of law practice problems, whether simulations or actual client issues, provide students the authenticity they need to construct meaningful understandings.

Finally, constructivists emphasize the role of social interaction in learning. Students engage in crucial mental activity when they negotiate meaning with each other. The hundreds of studies demonstrating the superiority of cooperative learning groups compared to all other teaching methods support this assertion. These groups are so effective because they allow students to obtain access to multiple perspectives with respect to a problem or issue and thereby to develop the more complex approaches and understandings required to address complicated problems.

Of course, such results are the product of groups who know how to work together, how to subdue ego in service of the goal of obtaining the best results possible, how to develop "positive interdependence," where each member of the group invests in the success of every other member of the group, and how to develop "accountability," where each member of the group holds every other member of the group responsible for performing her or his share of the group work. Chapter 6 addresses best practices for creating productive small group projects.

Adult Learning Theory

Adult learning theory has considerable overlap with the above theories but provides important points of emphasis. First, like constructivism, adult learning theory emphasizes the importance of real world experiences, but adult learning theory takes this idea one step further: not only must the experience be authentic, but the students must see the experience as authentic *and* as important to their personal and professional needs. Moreover, while adult learning theory and cognitivist theory share an emphasis on articulating learning goals, adult learning theory teaches us that students not only want to know what they need to be learning and how what they are learning relates their career goals, but also want to understand the relationship between the learning goals and the methods the teacher has chosen to achieve those goals. Like both cognitivism and constructivism, adult learning theory emphasizes the need for students to be in control of their own learning process. Students must have a role in deciding what and how they will learn. Finally, adult learning theory emphasizes the importance of teachers manifesting their respect for their students.

What We Know about Effective Teaching

Based on the research about teaching effectiveness in higher education, teaching excellence is measured by significant student learning. Teachers facilitate significant student learning when their teaching practices include expertise, respect, expectations, support, passion, preparation, variety, active learning, collaboration, clarity, and formative feedback.

Subject Matter Expertise

An essential foundation of good teaching is subject matter expertise. To teach well, we need to know doctrine, theory, policy, practical application, thinking skills, performance skills, ethical issues, and professionalism.

Respect

Mutual respect among students and teachers is fundamental to a healthy teaching and learning environment. Respect should go in three directions: teacher to students, students to teacher, and students to students. Classrooms that feature humiliation, intimidation, or denigration lead many students to withdraw from participation and learning.

Here's a brief list of behaviors that foster respect.

- Learn your students' names. Call students by name in and out of the classroom.
- Learn about your students' experiences and goals. Have students introduce themselves by completing a short questionnaire in class or on line.
- Value students' time. Law students, like their teachers, lead busy lives. Start and end class on time. Keep appointments with students. Respond to email from students.

- **Be inclusive.** We motivate students when we make them feel welcome and when we try to tie their learning to their personal and professional interests.
- **Model respect.** Respect is more about what we do than what we say. It is how we treat students, colleagues, and staff on a daily basis.

Expectations

Teachers' expectations greatly affect students' learning. High, realistic expectations lead to more student achievement; low expectations result in less student learning.

Five attributes of teacher expectations affect student motivation and learning: clarity, quality, achievability, uniformity, and credibility. Clarity requires us to define our expectations for both ourselves and our students. Quality means we need to emphasize quality rather than quantity. No course can teach all the skills and knowledge students need to develop; consequently, we should emphasize the critical skills and knowledge and accept we cannot teach everything. Achievability means our expectations should challenge students to stretch themselves and to do their best work while accounting for our students' current level of development and the demands of professional practice. Expectations are uniform if we communicate that we believe every student can attain a high level of achievement. Finally, our expectations are credible if we impose high expectations on ourselves. Perhaps the best way for teachers to inspire students to excellence is through modeling. We should have high expectations for ourselves. We should show, day after day, that we are diligently seeking continuous improvement in our professional practice.

Support

A supportive teaching and learning environment should accompany high expectations. We should demonstrate our commit-

ment to helping each student succeed in law school. A supportive environment is built upon teachers' attitudes, availability, and trust. One set of common descriptors of exemplary teachers focuses on their attitudes toward students — "helpful," "caring," "concerned," and "encouraging." Another group of attributes of effective teachers is "available," "accessible," and "approachable." Student-faculty contact outside of formal class time is associated with students' motivation, satisfaction, and active involvement in their own education. An operating assumption that reflects our trust is that "there is a good faith explanation for students' behavior." When we communicate our faith in students, most will reciprocate with faith in us.

Passion

Students regularly identify teachers' passion or enthusiasm as the most important ingredient of effective instruction. Our passion can inspire, energize, and motivate our students.

We should tell students directly what we love about teaching at this school, our joy in working with students, and our fascination with the subject matter. Celebrate success in the classroom. Provide positive reinforcement when students produce insight, solid analysis, or creative thinking. Teachers' nonverbal behaviors associated with enthusiasm include movement (away from the podium and out into the classroom), gestures, facial expressions, and smiling.

Preparation and Organization

Teachers and students benefit when they are clear about what should be learned, how that learning will take place, and how students will demonstrate their learning.

Preparation on the course design level includes: assessing our students' incoming strengths and weaknesses; establishing expectations for student attendance, preparation, participation, and behavior; planning our teaching methods, exercises, and assignments, both in and out of class; selecting print and electronic resources

that will support the teaching and learning activities; pacing the course rather than letting the clock or the calendar determine how fast and what we teach; designing opportunities for feedback to students throughout the course; and, of course, determining how student performance will be assessed and graded. Chapter 3 is devoted to course design.

A parallel set of issues inform our design of individual class sessions. Class session design includes: assessing where the students are at this point in the course in terms of their understanding and skills; selecting two, three, or four concepts or skills that students should learn or practice in the class session; deciding what students should do outside of class to prepare; planning what students will do during class; consciously choosing how the session will begin and end; and planning opportunities for teaching and student feedback about the students' learning. Chapter 4 addresses class session design.

However, effective teachers are not only prepared and organized; they are flexible too. Planning need not lead to rigidity. In every course and many individual class sessions, opportunities present themselves to explore a concept in more depth, weave in professionalism, and build on students' insights and skills.

Variety

We can inject variety into many aspects of our teaching —objectives, teaching and learning methods, materials, and evaluation. The extensive literature on learning styles makes clear that students prefer to learn in different ways. In addition, different types of teaching methods and materials are appropriate to achieve different objectives. Finally, variety can keep students' interest and sustain their motivation throughout a course.

Active Learning

Students learn from active and passive methods. Students learn passively when they listen to a presenter who organizes and conveys

information. Active learning occurs when students engage in more than listening. Law teachers employ many types of active learning techniques: Socratic dialogs, discussions, writing exercises, simulations, computer exercises, and real-life experiences in externships and clinics. Active learning is particularly effective in achieving four types of core goals of legal education: thinking skills, understanding concepts, lawyering skills, and professional values.

Collaboration

Two types of collaboration enhance teaching and learning in law school. The first is cooperative learning, where students work in pairs or small groups in or outside of class. Cooperative learning fosters the following: (1) more student learning and better academic performance, especially when the task is complex and conceptual; (2) development of problem solving, reasoning, and critical thinking skills; (3) positive student attitudes toward the subject matter and course; (4) closer relationships among students and between students and teachers; and (5) students' willingness to consider diverse perspectives.

The second is teacher and student collaboration in course design decisions. The benefit of teacher/student collaboration in course design is supported by the literature on learner-centered teaching, adult education theory, and empirical research on motivation and performance in college and law school. Student involvement in the design of their own education can increase students' intrinsic motivation and positive attitudes.

Clarity

Clarity in the classroom is *not* about "spoonfeeding" or "dumbing-down." Instead, it is about effectively communicating complex ideas, skills, and professional values. Several practices can help us communicate more clearly in the classroom, including roadmaps, closure, examples, visuals, and manifested openness to student questions.

Formative Feedback

Feedback is a critical element of teaching and learning. Formative feedback, which is designed to improve learning, is an essential part of the learning loop. Students engage in learning activities, show their learning in writing or orally, and then get feedback on how to improve their learning and performance. Effective formative feedback has four characteristics: specific, corrective, positive, and timely. Teachers should articulate *specific* criteria for student performance and give students feedback based on those criteria. *Corrective* feedback points out weaknesses in student work and provides strategies for improvement. *Positive* feedback identifies the strengths upon which students can build. *Timely* feedback comes relatively soon after student performance and gives students an opportunity to improve before their performance is evaluated.

Formative feedback is essential for teachers' continued development as well. To make appropriate adjustments during a course, we need to get feedback from students about their learning. A variety of Classroom Assessment Techniques (see Chapter 7) can give us that feedback. Further, for continuous improvement of our teaching practice, we can engage in self-reflection and gather input from students, consultants, and colleagues (see Chapter 8).

Chapter 2

Student Perspectives on Teaching and Learning

[T]o have the honor of being called a teacher-professor, you need to educate yourself about how to be an effective teacher.

Because good teaching focuses on student learning, we have included students' views about their legal education. **Students ask us to treat them with respect, engage them in learning, and help them become good lawyers.** They do not ask us to lower our expectations or "dumb down" their experience. In this chapter, we offer you students' words (in italics), mostly excerpts of students' comments taken from sixteen hours of videotaped interviews with sixty-seven students from seven different law schools. For ways to implement specific suggestions, see Chapters 3, 4, 5, 6, and 7.

Students Want to Be Treated with Respect

I learn better from professors that I feel talk with me and not down to me.

Students want us to treat them with compassion, welcome their different perspectives, create a positive and welcoming environment, and use their names. Respect is critical in the law school classroom.

Use Students' Names

[W]hen you raised your hand, it was not you in the back or you with the shirt, it was Ms. So and So or Mr. So and So. And it absolutely made you feel like all right the focus is on me and this professor wants to hear what I'm about to say.

Using students' names shows great respect. Students are delighted when teachers know their names and pronounce them correctly. Even if we can't learn all the names of our students in class, we can still have them available, on "name tents" placed in front students, on a seating chart, and we can use them in class discussions.

Treat Students as Colleagues

[I]t's not necessary for the professor to impress me by speaking in a mysterious language.... I'm already in awe of the professors. But I want to learn from a human being, a fellow human being.

Students frequently note that they learn more effectively from teachers whom they feel treat them as novice colleagues and who acknowledge their own fallibility. Our humanity empowers and motivates them; it does not make us appear weak. Being able to laugh at ourselves, admit mistakes, and acknowledge emotions help our students connect with us.

Include Different Perspectives in Class

I would advise a new professor [to] remember that he is teaching a group of people with varying cultural experiences and to actively solicit varying opinions so that the class is not dominated by a single culture.

Students want us to recognize how many different perspectives there are in the classroom, and seek to learn more about them.

They want us to be willing to talk about difficult issues of race, gender, sexual orientation, religion, and politics. They want us to realize that our references to sports and culture may be meaningless to them. On the other hand, diverse students may not want to be "spokespeople" for a certain perspective.

> *I'm in Criminal Law class where being one of two minority students in the class it seemed that every time that an issue of race came up that for some instant the professor always called on me as if I was the answer, you know, to everything. And sometimes I didn't mind it but then sometimes I did mind it because I didn't feel as though my purpose for being in that class was to answer all race issues that came up within that class.*

Create a Positive and Welcoming Environment

Teachers' and classmates' negative comments threaten students' confidence in their ability to grasp difficult material. They want us to maintain an enthusiastic, encouraging, and professional atmosphere.

> *I tend to learn better from professors that I respect and create that environment and make me feel that I can contribute to the profession. [W]hen [teachers] don't check a student that is talking out of line ... or if they don't maintain that kind of decorum ... it's very distracting to others ... since this is a professional environment ... there is a duty that teachers have of maintaining that.*

Creating a positive environment means that we also need to be careful about the assumptions we make about students.

> *[A]t least 99% [of us] try our hardest to make sure that we get it because we don't want to look foolish in class.... [I]t's very important that a teacher realize that ... we wouldn't ask the question in class ... unless we just honestly didn't understand it.*

Students Want to Be Engaged in Their Learning

The vast majority of students come to law school excited about becoming lawyers. They want assignments that relate to what happens in class. They seek to understand where the class is going and what they should take away at the end. Students want to be engaged in class. To help engage your students, ask not what **you** are doing, but what **they** are doing.

Use a Variety of Teaching Methods to Actively Engage Students

> [T]he more variation you can bring to class the more interested ... I stay. When it's just strictly lecture I tend to have a habit of drifting in and out.

Having a variety of teaching methods allows students to learn things in different ways, reaches students' diverse learning preferences, helps students solve legal problems from new angles, and mixes up the usual class performance patterns.

> [What] really helps in the process of the day-to-day going to class and getting something out of every class ... are varied, like workshop-type things.... Every day [one of my teachers] would [do] different types of exercises with the work.... getting involved in activities ... actually engaging in the classroom, you know, is a huge help.

Whether they are engaging in group work, role-plays, simulations, or working on other kinds of in-class exercises, students notice how much more they absorb when they are acting like lawyers in class.

> [A] thing that has really worked well for me and for other students is the problem method ... boy, is that helpful to kind of narrow the field down ... trying to figure out what

it is you're supposed to glean from this particular subject matter. [R]ole plays do help out a lot because ... it really gets it ingrained in your head because you're actively participating in things.

While such activities may limit the material we can expose our students to, our students' engagement during the activities will produce deeper understanding and what they learn will be far more memorable later. For suggestions on teaching techniques, refer to Chapters 3, 4, and 6.

Give Students an Organizational Structure — Provide Context for Learning

Students appreciate having a detailed syllabus and learning how a particular class fits into the course as a whole. In addition, previewing the class goals and materials at the beginning of class and summarizing them at the end help students stay on track and focus their learning.

[The teacher] gave roadmaps, what she described as the best way to understand the material. She would basically outline on the blackboard what it was that we were going to be doing in the next month and that gave us a very clear picture of what was expected, of what we were going to encounter, and it really summed up the material very well.

Make Class Preparation Assignments Reasonable and Meaningful

[W]hen you spend 3 or 4 hours preparing 25 pages of casebook material and the professor does not mention more than 3 of those pages in the entire hour ... it doesn't really encourage you to spend as much time and effort in preparing.

Assign students a manageable amount of reading—figure out how long it takes you to do the reading and expect that it will takes students longer. If you assign reading assignments of more than 40 pages, you may want to provide suggestions about how to approach the material. Consider assigning problems or hypotheticals in addition to cases and materials.

> [I]t would be far more productive to have small exercises that students can go and prepare for at home and then be engaged with other students. [I]f you gauge it back to 40 pages ... you can have more discussion and people will pick it up and then you can move on quicker than if you just did the 100 [pages] and everybody's crazy confused and asking fifty-million questions.

For more suggestions about making reasonable assignments, consult Chapter 4.

Provide Opportunities for Students to Work with Others

> Working in small groups facilitated discussion not possible in larger groups, and let all of us truly express ourselves without fear of being wrong or sounding dumb.

Students prefer to learn difficult material by working with others rather than in isolation. They learn a lot from verbally analyzing problems together and reading and commenting upon each other's work.

> Cooperative exercises and role playing exercises are very useful.... [A]t some point you're going to end up arguing and even if it's simply mediation ... those are practical models of what you will have to do.

Students appreciate being able to work with their classmates. When structured effectively, even the most introverted, small-group-work-resistant students realize the power of learning with and from their peers.

Be Aware of Students' Concerns about the Socratic Method

[T]he professors would ask questions and I would sit there and go what in the world are they asking?.... I had no idea what they wanted.

As with any technique, the Socratic method—engaging in a dialogue with students—can be effective or ineffective. Students who like the Socratic method value having to be prepared because they may be called upon, appreciate the opportunity to practice articulating arguments and responding to questions, and enjoy hearing from a greater range of classmates. Critics note how intimidating the Socratic method can be, how disruptive it is for those who learn from listening and writing rather than talking, and how it does not engage most of the class.

[P]rofessors that are good with the Socratic method.... blend in some enthusiasm that keeps you awake, and at the end of each point they clarify, well, that's not correct, or that's a good argument, but there's also this argument.

Students Want to Become Good Lawyers

The vast majority of our students plan to practice law and want to be good at it. They are eager to learn how our classes relate to their future careers. In their quest to become lawyers, students urge us to be clear about what we expect from them, offer opportunities to practice doing what we will be evaluating them on, provide feedback to help them improve, and allow multiple opportunities for them to show their progress in becoming good lawyers.

Connect What Students Are Learning to the Practice of Law

> *[M]y best experiences ... have been where professors actually gave you concrete examples of what is used in the real world ... actual trial transcripts ... or motions, things that we can put our hands on and say, "Okay, I understand what I'm doing now. I understand what we just spent the last month doing. I can see why we're doing this."*

Students are eager to hear about how our course connects to practice. For many of them, making direct connections to practice helps the law come alive.

> *I was in a firm with four people; two people would be attorneys, one would be one of our witnesses.... And we actually would really get involved, really figure out what exactly it is that we need to do, that we're going to have to once we get out of this place.... [T]hat class brought back my enthusiasm for wanting to go out and practice.... I want to sit here and practice law, and that's exactly what I was doing.*

Most of our students want to know how the material we teach relates to their future careers. We help students by giving them opportunities to connect class material to practice.

Be Explicit — Tell Students What You Expect and Give Them Opportunities to Practice

> *I think that an awful lot of times the professors start teaching a course without really knowing what they want the student to know at the end of the course.*

Students want to know how they can do well in our courses; that information helps them focus their studies on the knowledge, skills and values we want them to learn. Because our expectations are usually complex, it helps if we put our expectations in writing.

[Teachers]should tell us what they want.... [Y]ou find out after you get your test back.... [a]nd that's kind of too late.

Students note the discrepancy between what happens in class and how they earn their grades and appreciate when the two are congruent.

One of the most effective ways for me to prepare for my examinations ... was my professor brought in a fact pattern and we sat there in class and we worked through it. And that addresses issue spotting, brings up other sections to the pertinent law or cases.

[T]he classes where I think you take the most away from are where you have application.... although it does matter what grade you get ... the grade wasn't as important because I felt that I had learned something in that course.

Give Students Feedback on Their Progress

[F]eedback is absolutely critical and a lot of professors totally neglect it.... [Y]ou take exams or you write papers and some professors don't put comments on anything. And even if you've done well and there are no comments, it's impossible to learn how to do better or what, I mean, there had to have been shortcomings in your work at some point.

As novices, students struggle to accurately self-assess their learning. They want to know, "Am I getting it?" "Should I be trying new learning strategies?"

[The teacher] gave us a couple of hypotheticals to turn in. She didn't grade them but she commented upon them and that was very helpful.

Having opportunities to practice and get feedback is amazingly powerful for many students. As one student stated after being shown how to write an exam,

It was incredible. I felt calm. I felt powerful. I felt compe-
tent. I felt like yes, you can be a lawyer.

And when students don't do so well, we can still provide them
with positive reinforcement about their potential as lawyers.

[O]ne of the things that I think professors can empha-
size ... success in law isn't defined only by your grades in
law school, that people go on to do wonderful things ...
are employed and are happy, even though they weren't in
the top 10% of their class.

Allow Students to Show Their Progress in Multiple Ways

Most students do not want their grade based solely on a course's
final exam.

[T]he best classes that I've had have been ... [where] the
professors have them do different types of assignments for
a grade.... [T]he more chances ... that you can give stu-
dents is better, because some students are great orally, some
students are great on paper, some students do really well
with multiple choice.

Students' perspectives echo the experts': evaluating student performance on one graded event is not educationally sound. For more
on evaluating students, refer to Chapter 7.

Parting Shots — Students' General Advice to Us

[R]epeat things, slow down a little bit ... [you] forget
sometimes that we're just learning this stuff for the first
time.

[F]eel free to be yourself, to take chances, take risks, and to have fun because ... that's when the learning begins.

And perhaps the best advice:

Listen. Listen. That's all.

How to Hear *Your* Students' Perspectives

We encourage you to seek your students' views midway through each course. For suggestions on how you can gather and include students' perspectives, see Chapter 8.

Checklist for Considering the Students' Perspectives

Illustration 2-1 is a checklist you can use as you consider students' perspectives.

Illustration 2-1. Considering the Students' Perspectives Checklist

❏ **Students want to be treated with respect**
  ❏   Use students' names
  ❏   Treat students as colleagues
  ❏   Include different perspectives in class
  ❏   Create a positive and welcoming environment

❏ **Students want to be engaged in their learning**
  ❏   Use a variety of teaching methods and provide ways to students to be actively involved
  ❏   Give students an organizational structure
  ❏   Make assignments reasonable
  ❏   Allow students to work with others
  ❏   Be aware of problems with the Socratic method

❏ **Students want to become good lawyers**
  ❏   Connect learning to law practice
  ❏   Be explicit about what you expect
  ❏   Give students opportunities to practice
  ❏   Give feedback
  ❏   Allow students to show progress in multiple ways

Chapter 3

Designing the Course

Introduction

Chapter 3 marks a transition in this book. Chapters 1 and 2 focused on theory and on understanding law students; this chapter and all of those that follow translate years of research on effective teaching into a set of concrete suggestions.

In this chapter, we offer ideas for designing courses. Most broadly, course design is a recursive process, as reflected in Illustration 3-1, in which you: (1) identify the skills, knowledge, and values you want your students to learn ("course goals"); (2) evaluate your students' incoming knowledge, skills, and values ("assess learners"); (3) decide how you will assess (a) whether students have attained the course goals and (b) whether your course design decisions are good ones, and then (c) design appropriate assessments ("plan assessment"); (4) select texts; (5) design the course to help the students achieve the course goals, which includes writing the syllabus ("design the course"); (6) design a course webpage ("design course web")—if you are going to do so; (7) implement the design ("implement design"); (8) evaluate the course design ("evaluate course"); and, finally, (9) using the information you gained from evaluating the course, redesign the course according to the same process.

We have organized the rest of this chapter according to the timeline suggested by Illustration 3-1.

Illustration 3-1. The Recursive Course Design Process

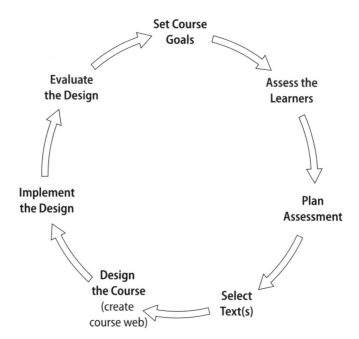

Initiating the Design Process: Setting Course Goals

A goal is a statement of what students should be able to do by the end of your course. Goals influence which topics you teach, what you expect of your students, how you design your syllabus, class sessions, examinations, and paper assignments.

A good place to start in identifying goals is thinking about what you can do in this field *because* you are an expert. Another way is to imagine your students a few years after they have taken your course. What do you hope the students have retained from the course? We encourage you to be ambitious in describing your course goals—think beyond the limits of your assigned course label (e.g., pre-trial practice, environmental law). Aspire to produce learning that transcends. Limit yourself to three or four learning goals per course, and focus not on what students should know but, rather, what they should be able to do.

All courses involve a mix of higher-level goals and lower-level thinking skills. In the law school context, higher-level skills include: drafting law-related documents, analyzing and solving legal problems, evaluating cases, conducting client and witness interviews, etc. These higher-level skills implicate lower level skills such as knowing and being able to explain the applicable law, and generating factual, legal and policy arguments.

Know Your Students: Assessing the Learners

The most common error committed by law professors is assuming their students are like them. In fact, recent studies suggest law professors are more like each other and much less like their students in terms of the characteristics that might influence designing a law school course. This difference between law professors and students is exacerbated because our own law school experiences were several years ago. Law professors also often have different learning style preferences than their students. Unlike most law professors, many law students enjoy learning through collaboration with others, prefer visually-focused learning experiences and prefer to learn in the context of simulated law practice activities. Of course, law students also tend to vary among themselves in their learning preferences. In short, we cannot assume that our students enjoy learning the way we did.

Plan Assessment: How Will You Know Whether Your Students Are Learning?

Thinking about assessment before you start designing your course may seem counter-intuitive. You may even worry that, if you were to design assessment instruments before you designed your course, you might end up "teaching to the test." Educational experts, however, recognize that designing assessment right after you have articulated your objectives and before you design your course ensures that your assessment instruments are congruent with your goals.

In fact, the process of designing the assessment should and often does influence course goals and objectives. Even more significantly, designing your assessment instruments and revising your goals will (and should) influence how you design your course. Your assessment instruments should focus on assessing student learning of the skills you regard as most important, and you should be designing your course so that you and your students devote the greatest amount of time and effort to developing those skills.

Finding the Book of Your Dreams: Sifting the Morass to Find the Right Textbook for You

Start by surveying others who teach your subject or ask a colleague, but, as tempting as it is to follow the majority, we suggest you dig deeper. *The core principle in selecting a textbook is finding the book that best furthers as many of your course goals as possible without undermining any of your other course goals.* A good textbook for you is one that makes it easier for you to help your students develop the skills, knowledge and values you hope to teach them. Illustration 3-2 is a tool to help you consider the most significant textbook selection considerations.

Illustration 3-2. Textbook Evaluation Tool

Author(s) Title Publisher	Congruence with Your Objectives	Case Selection and Sequencing	Quality and Quantity of Problems	Quality and Quantity of Questions	Teacher's Manual: Assessment Help	Teacher's Manual: Teaching Help
Text #1:						
Text #2:						
Text #3:						

Designing the Course So Students Will Learn What You Want Them to Learn

This discussion focuses on the guiding principles of course design. As you consider these suggestions in the light of your own course planning efforts, keep your list of learning objectives and assessments by your side. As the discussion below reflects, the learning objectives and assessments will guide your course design decisions.

Start by dividing your overall learning goals into at least five and as many as eight or nine sub-categories, called "learning units." We cannot encourage you enough to avoid obsessing over coverage. Avoid sacrificing effectiveness on the altar of coverage. While we encourage you to develop a list of doctrinal categories, we discourage you from limiting your sub-category list to doctrine. If your course goals include developing your students' ability to engage in problem-solving in your field, you need to prioritize teaching time for this skill.

The most valuable thing you can provide to students is practice and feedback. New learners in a field need learning experiences that allow them to practice applying each of the concepts and principles in isolation *and* they need instruction and practice in combing those concepts and principles and procedures to analyze complex problems that implicate multiple doctrinal areas. In other words, your case-book may need supplementation. You may need to provide students with readings and other materials specifically directed to the problem-solving tasks in which they will be engaging (e.g., readings on conducting client interviews or drafting pleadings or contracts).

In terms of class preparation assignments, the research strongly suggests that students learn more and learn it better when they read cases for the purpose of solving a problem, and students are more likely to give skills reading assignments the required attention if those assignments are situated in a simulated law practice problem. The research also suggests law students learn more from cases when they possess relevant prior knowledge *before* they begin reading. Consequently, consider providing or assigning introductory readings.

Moreover, students learn more when they engage in deep processing of the materials. By expanding your conception of the term "assignments" and therefore explicitly assigning tasks in addition to reading a list of assigned cases and statutes, you can engage your students in a wide spectrum of intellectually-challenging processing activities, including:

- developing a theory that explains the need for the doctrine;
- synthesizing the reading assignments with past assignments;
- comparing a case or series of cases to an existing or proposed statute;
- developing examples and non-examples of a concept addressed in their readings;
- analyzing hypotheticals;
- generating hypothetical problems;
- drafting a pleading or contract clause designed to address the problem; or
- drafting a proposed statute to address a problem raised by a line of cases.

Thinking through the kinds of activities in which you want your students to engage is crucial because you want to be sure that you maximize your classroom time with students. Educational experts frequently talk in terms of selecting the best medium for delivering a particular aspect of students' learning. Available instructional media include: texts, live teachers, computer programs, websites, videotapes, podcasts, and small group experiences. Live teachers, in comparison to all alternative media of instruction, are uniquely flexible and adaptable and uniquely possess empathy. Live teachers can be the best instructional medium for inspiring learners and possess the unique ability to teach by functioning as role models. Consequently, you need to be making conscious decisions about what aspects of your teaching require your physical presence and what aspects can be moved to another instructional medium.

Having decided how you will structure each individual learning unit, you are ready to consider how you will combine the units to design your course. As you begin this synthesis process, keep the following considerations in mind.

First, consider how best to sequence your learning units and, within each learning unit, consider how best to sequence students' progress through that unit. Don't assume the author of your casebook knows best. Students prosper most when their learning experiences are challenging but not overwhelming and when the professor gradually increases the difficulty of the intellectual challenge in the course. Sequencing also is a matter of prioritizing. Many of us teach our courses as if the most important topics are the ones with which we start and the least important are those at the end. In fact the opposite may be true. And students learn little when, in an effort to "finish" our syllabus, we abandon all semblance of active engagement, use lecture format all the time, and move through the materials like tanks through wet paper.

Second, consider the burden you are imposing on the students, their competing obligations in other courses, and the importance of school-life balance for your students.

Third, make sure you consciously sequence your course for variety. Variety allows us to retain our students' attention and cater to every student's learning preference. For example, your law practice problems should engage students in the wide spectrum of activities in which lawyers engage, including arguing, evaluating, reading, drafting, re-writing, negotiating, communicating with others (clients, colleagues, other lawyers, judges), interviewing, planning, and presenting.

Finally, carefully plan how you will begin and end your course. Beginnings should help students see what is exciting about your course. Endings should provide students with opportunities to reflect on what they have learned and consider how they will use it.

Writing Your Syllabus

Your syllabus can be just a list of assignments. But it also can be culture-making. In many instances, our first interaction with our students occurs via the course syllabus. Our syllabi can engage students, inspire their confidence and interest in you and your subject, communicate your investment in their success, display your professionalism as a teacher, demonstrate your skill in planning the course, and establish high expectations. Your syllabus also can leave students cold or, worse yet, discouraged, disinterested, disengaged, anxious, confused, and hostile.

Syllabus construction is mostly a matter of science and careful decision-making, but it is also art. The science suggests you should address certain topics in your syllabus and follow best practices in addressing those topics. At the same time, your syllabus communicates a lot about you: based on your syllabus, your students will draw inferences about who you are and how you will teach.

Your syllabus serves as a contract between you and the students. It defines your relationship, establishes your respective rights, and creates your respective responsibilities. As with any contract, problems arise if the obligations it describes are ambiguous or if either party asserts rules or expectations not articulated in the writing. Consequently, make sure you have a colleague read your syllabus before you distribute it to students.

Syllabi should provide the basic information students need and should address all the issues that reasonably might arise in the class, including:

- your name and contact information, and your office hours, and appointments;
- the name of the course, the required texts, and a description of the course;
- attendance and timely arrival for class;
- course goals, statement of teaching philosophy, and teaching methods;
- expectations for class preparation and other classroom conduct;
- schedule of class meetings, readings, projects, and other assignments;
- grading, late assignments, and failures to complete assigned projects; and
- plagiarism and/or any other forms of academic misconduct that may arise in your class.

If you have a course webpage, your syllabus should provide information about accessing it and your policies for using it. (Some institutions mandate the inclusion of certain additional information in syllabi, such as the institution's mission statement, information about disability accommodations, and other such matters. Check with your institution.)

Consider also the degree to which you wish to give yourself leeway to modify policies stated in your syllabus. If you wish to retain the ability to modify your course policies or assignments, be sure your syllabus communicates that you can do so. You either can have a general caveat explaining that the syllabus is subject to change or specifically address areas where change is a genuine possibility. For example, if you wish to retain the right to modify your final exam, you can say, "The format of the final exam is subject to change."

For many students, the schedule of class assignments and the grading policies are the only sections they carefully read.

Students want specific details about when and how the professor expects them to fulfill their scholastic duties. Your schedule should include all assignments and projects, the dates they are due, and the dates of any exams. Organize these elements by topic rather than by chapter or page numbers. Clarity is crucial. A clear course road map provides each student an opportunity to formulate a "plan of attack" that compliments his or her learning preference. At the same time, both students and professors prefer the professor retain some discretion to modify the assignments after the semester begins. An easy way to retain this flexibility is by including a disclaimer at the beginning of this section of your syllabus that states "To maximize student learning in this class, I may need to adjust the assignments. I promise to give you at least one week's notice before implementing any such change."

Students also need and deserve to know what weight will be placed on the various graded activities in the course and whether other factors such as class participation and course webpage contributions will be factored into their grades. It is particularly useful to provide students with guidance about the standards by which you will be evaluating their work. Such grading rubrics (see Chapter 7 for additional information) help eliminate confusion and concerns over the accuracy or fairness of grading. If your students will be handing in work, make sure you also communicate policies addressing what happens if students hand in assignments late or not at all.

Finally, before you start writing any of the sections, think carefully about the overarching messages you wish to communicate to your students. Students will draw inferences about who you are, what you value, what you think of your students, and how you will teach based solely on what you say in your syllabus and the tone with which you say it. For example, you may find it helpful to include some self-deprecating humor in your syllabus. Many law students experience law professors as arrogant. You also should ask a lot of your students, communicate confidence in your ability to teach, and express confidence in your students' ability to learn. Because teacher enthusiasm facilitates student learning, your syllabus should express enthusiasm for your subject.

Because law students are adult learners (for the most part), one of the best things you can do to enhance their learning experience is to share your power to establish course policies. By ceding some power to students, you convey important messages about your sense of the students' competence, autonomy, and abilities. You also show that you have faith in and respect for them and that you have confidence in your own ability to synthesize their needs and the course goals. The easiest facet of your syllabus for sharing control is course coverage. Select those topics you regard as essential and then let your students select from among the remaining topics. All three of us also have found it easy to allow students to articulate their expectations of us and to suggest teaching methods they would like us to include in our repertoire. You can also ask students to develop or contribute to your list of student expectations and for input into your grading scheme.

Evaluate the Design and Plan for the Future

Having designed the course, created a syllabus and set up a course webpage, the next logical step, of course, would be to implement, i.e., teach, the course. If you have adopted the recommendations of this book, your course design has embedded multiple assessments so that throughout the semester, you are gathering data about how well your students are learning and, where possible, adjusting the design of your course.

Ideally, the goal in course evaluation and redesign is to be systematic, reflective and continuous. Your approach is systematic to the extent that the information you strive to develop from your efforts at assessing your students' learning covers the breadth and depth of skills, knowledge and values you teach and evaluates student learning of all learning objectives. Your evaluation process is reflective if you devote time and effort to reflecting (in a teaching journal for example) on each class session and on the results of your efforts at assessment. Finally, the word "continuous" conveys the idea that your efforts should continue throughout the semester and with respect to each offering of your course. The idea is analogous to the continuous improvement model in business planning. In both contexts, data is used to inform future planning and each implementation is treated as an opportunity to improve.

Checklist for Course Design Process

Illustration 3-3 is a checklist you can use as you work through the course design process.

Illustration 3-3. Course Design Process Checklist

❑   Determine what you want students to know, value, and be able to do

❑   Figure out who your students are

❑   Decide how you will assess students and draft assessments

❑   Choose texts

❑   Design each part of the course

❑   Design the course as a whole

❑   Create a syllabus that
  ❑   provides the basic information students need and addresses all the issues that reasonably might arise in the class
  ❑   engages students
  ❑   communicates high expectations
  ❑   includes challenging and appropriate reading and problem-solving assignments
  ❑   paces the course carefully to make sure the course has an engaging opening and an effective closing and avoids the end-of-semester rush
  ❑   devotes instructional time to problem-solving instruction and experiences

❑   Create a course webpage (if you have decided to have one)

❑   Implement your design

❑   Evaluate your design

You will find examples of the concepts from this chapter in Appendix 3 on the book's website — http://lawteaching.org/resources/ books/teachinglawbydesign/teachinglawbydesign-appendices.pdf.

Appendix 3-1: Course Goals

Appendix 3-2: Lesson Objectives

Appendix 3-3: Syllabi

Chapter 4

Designing Each Class Session

Law school class sessions can lead to significant student learning and teacher satisfaction if you adopt an intentional approach to class design. We recommend a five-step class design process, reflected in Illustration 4-1. We recognize that this process is more elaborate than most law teachers' class planning, but many teachers implicitly engage in much of the process. Even if the entire process is not for you, you can improve your teaching and your students' learning by expanding your class design efforts in any of the elements described below.

Illustration 4-1. Five-Step Class Design Process

Context

Each class occurs in a larger context, which includes important background aspects of the course, the students, and the teacher. Analyzing the context should consume very little of the teacher's planning time. All we need to do is spend a few minutes thinking about the context before we move on to the rest of the class design process.

Course Context

Law schools may mandate that certain concepts or skills be taught in required courses to prepare students for subsequent courses, the bar exam, or practice. Elective courses may provide faculty members with more options. Time, scheduling and place in the course also influence class planning. Designing a class that meets for an hour three times per week in the morning should differ from a class that meets once per week for three hours at night. Where the class fits in the life of the course has a significant influence on class design as well.

Student Context

Our students' needs and motivation change as they progress through law school. Most first-semester, first-year students are interested in their courses and eager to learn. Second and third-year law students may display less interest in their courses but are eager to graduate, pass the bar exam, and begin their careers. They may respond well to a class with content and skills that are directly relevant to law practice, such as preparing a will. Similarly, students' previous exposure to the material will affect class design, as will their real world experience with the subject. In addition, the numbers of students affects course design.

A variety of active learning methods and feedback are essential elements of successful class sessions regardless of the size of the class; nevertheless, enrollment affects the objectives, instructional activities, material, and feedback for a class.

Teacher Context

We all have strengths and weaknesses as teachers. We are more comfortable with some teaching methods, content, and skills than others. In designing classes, we should build on our strengths and address our weaknesses. Classes that address content and skills with which we are comfortable may be appropriate to experiment with new learning and feedback activities. On days when we are on shakier ground or are struggling with other matters, we may choose to stick with the tried and true.

Class Objectives

Objectives are the foundation on which each class should be built. The number of objectives appropriate for a single class session depends on all of the context issues above. In general, we favor depth over breadth and significant learning over coverage. Consequently, one to three class objectives are generally appropriate for a one-hour class session.

The objectives for each class should have three basic characteristics. They should:

- Be learner, rather than teacher, centered;
- Encompass a broad range of professional knowledge, skills, and values; and
- Be clear and concrete.

Learner Centered

Learner-centered objectives focus on what students will learn, rather than what the teacher will do or cover in class. To focus on student learning, begin class objectives with the phrase "As a result of this class, students will be able to." Then, complete each objective with the knowledge, skills, or values that students should learn in the class session. For example, rather than having the class objective be to get through 20 pages of material, cover three cases, discuss four problems, present an analytical framework or demonstrate a skill, your class objective could be: "As a result of this class, students will be able to use six components of statutory interpretation to analyze problems involving statutes and regulations."

Professional Knowledge, Skills, and Values

Because success as a lawyer rests on a set of knowledge, skills, and values, class objectives should focus on students learning and practicing knowledge, skills, and values related to the course. As we design a class session, we should focus on the critical knowledge, skills, or values. Choosing and articulating class objectives helps us make those choices intentionally.

For most law school courses, knowledge includes legal doctrine, policy, and theory. An individual class session will focus on a small subset of the relevant knowledge for the course. In addition to case analysis, statutory analysis, problem solving, or critical thinking, we should include other skills lawyers need to succeed in practice. For example, one well-respected report lists ten "Fundamental Lawyering Skills": problem solving, legal analysis and reasoning, legal research, fact investigations, oral and written communication, counseling, negotiation, litigation and alternative dispute resolution, organization and management of legal work, and recognizing and resolving ethical dilemmas. Professional attributes and values are perhaps the most overlooked aspect of traditional legal education. Yet lawyers consistently identify a number of aspects of professionalism as important to success in law practice, including honesty, integrity, reliability, responsibility, judgment, diligence, tolerance, self-motivation, empathy, and respect for clients, lawyers, judges, and staff. We should look for opportunities to include values in our class objectives.

Clear and Concrete

The key to clear and concrete class objectives is to focus on observable student behavior. We can't observe students "understanding" a concept or "appreciating" a value. We can observe students laying out the analytical framework for an area of law, identifying legal issues in a fact pattern, or demonstrating respect for other students in the classroom.

Although we believe deeply in the importance of articulating class objectives, we believe their form is flexible. Our class objectives are the answers to: "What are the few 'essentials' in terms of knowledge, skills, or values that the students should have when they leave this class session?" Those answers should drive our design of instructional activities, feedback, and materials.

Instructional Activities

Effective class planning requires designing what we will do during the class and what our students will do. For design purposes, we divide the instructional activities in class into three sections: (1) opening—the first one to five minutes; (2) body—the bulk of the class period; and (3) closing—the final one to five minutes.

Opening

The first few minutes of a class can be the most valuable. Our opening can grab attention, motivate, communicate objectives, and build a bridge to previous learning. We can plan to gain students' attention in many different ways—a projected image relevant to the subject for that day, a mental challenge represented by an overarching question for the lesson, a news story, or by celebrating student success. Once we have students' attention, we should motivate them to engage by communicating our own passion for the subject or by showing students how the concepts or skills for the class will be relevant and valuable to them in their personal lives, on the bar exam, or in practice.

Share class objectives with the students to focus student learning. When students know what they need to be learning, they can devote their effort to the essentials, rather than tangential matters. Finally, plan the transition from previous classes. Put the day's class in the larger context of the course. Help students see the big picture by using a diagram or example to show them how to fit the lesson into the rest of the course.

Body

The primary design decision for the body of the class is selecting teaching and learning methods. Use one overarching principle — choose methods to maximize student learning of class objectives. Teaching and learning methods such as Socratic dialogue, lecture, or simulations are not "good" or "bad" methods. They are tools to facilitate student learning and their appropriateness varies according to class objectives.

Two subsidiary considerations are relevant to our choice of teaching and learning methods — learning styles and depth of learning. Below, we summarize and apply Fleming and Mills' sensory-based learning style model, which identifies four learning style preferences. Illustration 4-2 identifies the four styles and examples of teaching learning methods that are most comfortable for each style.

The learning styles literature does not suggest we plan methods to address each learning style in each class. But because students prefer to learn in various ways, we should plan to use more than one method for each class session and should incorporate many methods over the life of the course. In fact, evidence suggests that all students benefit from learning in ways with which they are less comfortable. Empirical research supports the value of using a variety of teaching methods. In general students remember about 10% of what they read, 20% of what they hear, and 30% of what they see in pictures or graphics. With two senses or methods, student retention improves. Students remember approximately 50% of what they see and hear. Since speaking involves both active cognition and hearing, students retain about 70% of what they say. Couple speaking with doing and retention soars to 90%. Illustration 4-3 presents this information graphically.

In every course, some content and skills are more important than others. We should design instructional activities that involve

Illustration 4-2. Sensory Based Learning Styles

Learning Style	Teaching/Learning Methods
Digital • Learn via reading and writing • Logical, deductive reasoning • Abstract thinkers • Find patterns and organization	• Read to prepare for class • Brief cases • Write responses to problems • Outline course • Lecture — listen and take notes
Auditory • Learn via hearing and speaking • Process and store information chronologically • Memory aided by mnemonic devices	• Socratic dialogue • Large group discussion • Small group problem solving • Debate • Listen to stories, cases, hypotheticals
Visual • Learn via sight • Organize concepts through spatial relationships • Store ideas graphically	• Visual tools of all types — whiteboard, pictures, videos, handouts, slides • Diagrams, flow charts, graphs, concept maps
Kinesthetic • Learn by doing • Store knowledge as experience • Attend to physical and emotional manifestation of concepts	• Simulations and role plays • Authentic law practice experiences, including service learning, clinical, and externship experiences • Real documents — pleadings, contracts, deeds

multiple senses and methods for the most important aspects of the course. For example, if a significant learning objective is for students to be able to apply the law, policy, and strategy involved in creating security agreements, we may ask students to read applicable sections of the Uniform Commercial Code, discuss cases or problems applying those sections, review a sample security agreement, and draft a security agreement for a hypothetical or real client.

Illustration 4-3. Senses, Methods, and Retention

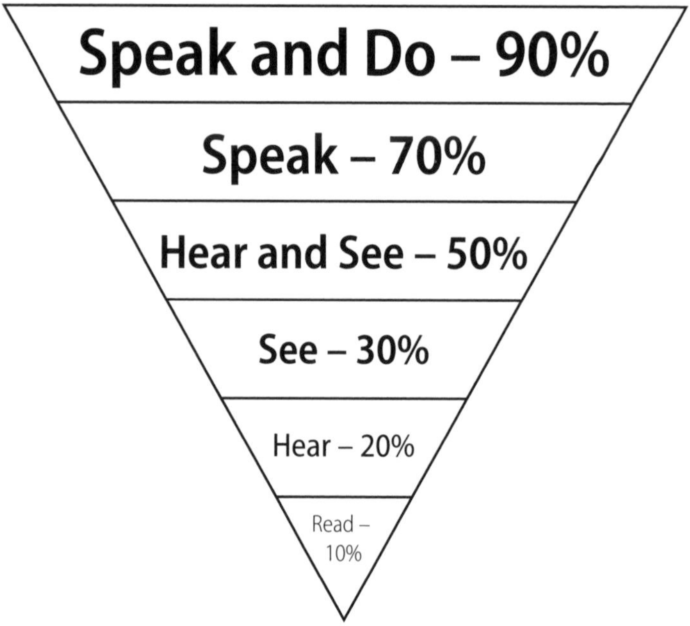

Closing

The last few minutes of class can include significant learning. We can plan the last few minutes of class to review, summarize, transfer learning, provide feedback, conduct classroom assessment, and re-motivate students.

Students need to consolidate new learning. We can review and comment briefly on the class objectives or articulate the few essential concepts, skills, or values students should have grasped in the class. With a graphic projected on a screen or with a handout, we could demonstrate how the doctrine, theory, or skills fit in the larger scheme or analytical framework. Students can play an active role in the closing by voicing the key concepts they learned in that class or by completing a diagram or chart that draws together the learning for that day. We can facilitate transfer of learning and re-motivate students by showing how the knowledge, skills, and values learned during a class will be valuable in the remainder of the course, on the bar exam, or in the profession after graduation.

Feedback

Feedback is crucial to effective teaching and learning and should be a part of our course design, class planning, and the teaching/learning activities we use with our students. As we design class sessions, we should look for ways to incorporate formative feedback, feedback designed to help students improve. By the end of the course, feedback should have been part of many class sessions, having occurred at various points in a class session.

- **Opening.** Feedback is an excellent way to gain students' attention and to build a bridge to prior learning. Class could begin with a short multiple-choice quiz that addresses key concepts from a prior classes and important aspects of the current class. The quiz could be on a handout, a slide, or with a "clicker" system. Immediate feedback should follow the quiz.
- **Body.** During the bulk of the class period, feedback can vary from simple to elaborate. For example, when a student performs a skill well, we can call attention to it briefly—"Jan just synthesized a line of cases by ..." or "Fran drafted an excellent set of interrogatories that...." Or we could spend half of a class period going over the rubric for a practice exam and involving students in assessing their exam performance.
- **Closing.** By reviewing the class objectives or summarizing the major points for the class (done either by the teacher or students), the students get feedback on the critical content, skills, and values they should have learned that day. Or the class could end with a problem that integrates the learning for that day—feedback on the appropriate analysis could be imme-

diate, happen via the course web page, or be part of the opening of the next class.
- **After class.** Feedback on quizzes, problems, hypotheticals,
outlines, etc can take place in a discussion on the course web
page, via an applicable CALI exercise, or one-on-one in the
teacher's office. We believe that a primary obligation of effective teachers is to provide feedback to students. For more
on feedback and assessment, see Chapter 7.

Materials

Materials include both print and electronic resources that students will use outside of class or that students and teachers will use
during class. Examples include readings, websites, pictures, videos,
computer exercises, handouts, slides, objects, and items written
on the board.

We can choose and design materials to achieve our objectives, guide
student preparation, support other instructional activities, and facilitate feedback. These four functions of materials provide guidance on the types of materials we should select for each class.
Different class objectives, instructional activities, and feedback call
for different types of materials. Several additional considerations apply
regardless of the type of material. Effective materials are selective,
variable, focused, and interactive.

Selective. For virtually any topic we address in class, we could
find thousands of pages of text (cases, statutes, articles) along with
websites, pictures, and videos. Consequently, for every class session, we are choosing a tiny slice of the available material. What
should guide those choices? First, we should select the material that
is most relevant to our class objectives. Second, we should limit
the material we assign to students to a reasonable amount. We believe that two hours of student preparation for each hour of class
is reasonable. Selectivity applies to our use of materials during class
as well. Research shows that students will copy verbatim anything

we write on the board or project on a screen. A few key phrases or a clear, simple flow chart will aid student learning more than a board covered with our writing or slides jammed with text.

Variable. Variety in materials is a virtue for several reasons. In modern life, we get information from both print and electronic sources. Our class materials should reflect that reality. We miss opportunities to enhance our students' learning if we march through the casebook without incorporating relevant stories, documents, and images. Further, variety makes our classes more interesting. Each time we shift material in the classroom, we grab attention.

Focused. One way to facilitate student preparation for class is to provide questions about the material before class. These questions allow students to focus their preparation, just as a lawyer prepares for the issues that will be central to a motion hearing. We ask many other questions in class as well, just as judges ask lawyers questions in court. We can provide the advance questions to students in writing via a supplement, webpage, email, or a handout. Focus questions can address doctrine, skills, and values. We can use focus devices in material we prepare for use in class. For example, we can focus student's attention in handouts and on slides through text boxes, bullets, numbering, font, symbols, or color.

Interactive. Much of the material we assign to students is designed for students to read, such as cases, statutes, and articles. Likewise, materials we use in class are often intended for students to read or view, including slides, handouts, pictures, and diagrams. This type of material is valuable for presenting doctrine, policy, analytical frameworks, and theory to students. To maximize the effectiveness of material in achieving class objectives, we should look for ways to make materials interactive as well.

Simple techniques can add interactive features to many types of materials.

- **Readings.** The most passive use of readings is to simply assign pages. We can encourage more active reading by giving students focus questions (discussed above) or by asking students to do something with the reading—brief a case, apply a statute to a problem, or synthesize the law and policy from the material.

- **Videos.** Short video clips relevant to the class objectives can be powerful instructional tools. Videos are readily available on websites such as www.youtube.com. Books such as *Reel Justice* describe portions of movies that illustrate doctrine, skills, and values.
- **Slides.** Presentation software, such as PowerPoint, allows us to produce slides that transmit information and images to students. These visual aids are helpful to many students. However, if we use slides extensively and the slides do no more than present information, many students will become passive receivers. We can change this dynamic by including slides with questions, problems, quizzes, and hypotheticals designed to facilitate active student engagement in the classroom.
- **Whiteboards, flip charts, and projectors.** These basic tools excel at supporting discussions. We can easily capture student contributions to class discussions on the whiteboard, a chart, or a document projector.
- **Word processing software.** We can accomplish the interactive aspects of presentation software and whiteboards by projecting a document on a screen in word processing software.
- **Diagrams, flow charts, and tables.** These tools can be excellent devices to organize concepts and illustrate the interrelationships among ideas. Better yet, we can provide students with partially completed or blank diagrams and tables and have students complete them before or during class.
- **Handouts.** We can accomplish many of the functions of materials with handouts, distributed in either paper or electronic form. The interactivity of a handout we design for use during class depends in part on how we incorporate white space. Studies compared the learning results of (1) students given the professor's notes, (2) students given a barebones outline into which they can take notes, and (3) students given nothing. The students in group (2) learned the most and the students in group (1) and (3) learned at about the same level.

Evaluate and Revise

We encourage you to engage in a systematic, reflective, continuous process for evaluating and revising class designs. After class, spend five minutes reflecting. Were the class objectives achieved? How effective were the opening and closing? The teaching and learning activities? Did you provide feedback to students? Were the materials appropriate and effective? Memorialize your reflections in writing and keep them someplace that you will not lose them, such as with your notes for the class or in a teaching log.

The next time you teach the class, begin your preparation by reviewing your reflections. Then, after considering the new context that will apply the next time you teach the class, make appropriate revisions in the objectives, instructional activities, feedback devices, and materials.

There is no such thing as a perfect class session and we do not seek perfection in our classes. Instead, we strive to make incremental improvements in our classes over time. The class design process helps improve teaching and enhance students' learning class-by-class.

Checklist for Class Design Process

Illustration 4-4 is a checklist you can use as you work through the class design process.

Illustration 4-4. Class Design Process Checklist

❏ **Consider the context of the class**
   ❏ Course context
   ❏ Student context
   ❏ Teacher context

❏ **Draft learner-centered, clear, concrete class objectives**
   ❏ Knowledge (doctrine, theory)
   ❏ Professional skills (thinking, performance)
   ❏ Professional values

❏ **Choose instructional activities to achieve class goals**
   ❏ Opening
   ❏ Body (teaching/learning activities)
   ❏ Closing

❏ **Provide feedback to students**

❏ **Select materials**
   ❏ Use outside class (readings, CALI, Internet)
   ❏ Use in class (slides, whiteboard, videos, diagrams, handouts)

❏ **Evaluate your design**

You will find examples of the concepts from this chapter in Appendix 4 on the book's website—http://lawteaching.org/resources/books/teachinglawbydesign/teachinglawbydesign-appendices.pdf.

Appendix 4-1: Charts, Tables, and Diagrams
    Dismissal under FRCP 41 Chart
    Chart Depicting Restitution in the Context of a
        Contracts Course
    Common Contract Terms Chart
    Personal Jurisdiction Analytical Framework
    Partially Completed Graphic Organizer Synthesizing
        Contract
    Interpretation Principles

Chapter 5

Student Motivation, Attitudes, and Self-Regulation

Introduction

"It's easy to teach 1Ls. But how do you motivate burnt-out 3Ls?"

"One day in class, I called on three students, and none of them were prepared. I just wanted to walk right back out of the room! What else could I do?"

"I want my students to develop a sense of professionalism and a commitment to the lawyer's responsibility to serve the community. But how do you teach values?"

"My students just want to be spoon-fed. They don't want to do any of the work for themselves. How do I get my students to take control over their own learning?"

We often hear smart, dedicated law teachers express concerns about motivating their students, about changing or developing student attitudes and values, and about training law students to be self-motivated, reflective, lifelong learners. This chapter addresses these concerns from several perspectives.

Motivating Students

Introduction

Motivating students arguably is not really its own, separate subject but, a natural outgrowth of adopting the good teaching principles we describe in this book.

Educational experts describe the goal of motivation instruction as increasing the likelihood that students achieve the state known as "flow." In the academic context, flow refers to a mental and emotional state in which the student experiences a task as exciting and challenging yet attainable. The student feels confident yet pressed to grow, engaged yet not over-stimulated. Students who feel a sense of flow immerse themselves in the learning process. They feel less inhibited than normal and also feel in control. Even though the work may be challenging, they experience the work as effortless. In many instances, a student who experiences flow is so engaged in the learning process the student loses track of time. Most of us have had at least a few class sessions in which both we and our students have lost ourselves in the thrill of learning. Wouldn't it be great to have more such sessions? How can we systematically and reflectively teach for flow?

Experts draw an important distinction between teacher efforts fostering students' extrinsic motivation and efforts designed to help students find intrinsic motivation. Extrinsic motivation emphasizes things teachers do to reward student engagement and to impose natural consequences for student disengagement. Extrinsic motivational ploys include emphasizing grades, administering pop quizzes, and considering class participation in students' grades.

While extrinsic factors can influence motivation, they seldom produce the long-range satisfaction and sustained interest possible when students are intrinsically motivated. In educational settings, intrinsic motivation refers to qualities and circumstances within the student or the learning activity that stimulate engagement in a course. Recent studies have focused on techniques teachers can use to stimulate the development of intrinsic student interest. These studies, taken together, prescribe a wide variety of choices for inspiring and motivating students, which we describe below.

Specific Techniques

Teacher Attitudes That Motivate Students

Teacher passion and confidence significantly influence student motivation. As we explain in chapters 1, 2, and 6, students frequently describe their most inspiring teachers as passionate about their subjects and about student learning and confident in themselves and in their students' ability to learn. These attitudes help students discover the excitement that led their professors to become law teachers in the first place and to feel confident in their ability to learn what we want them to learn. Teachers can show passion for student learning by expressing excitement about students' insights, by making themselves available to students, by actively and explicitly looking for new ways to help students learn, and by treating student learning as the principle goal in their classes. If a student suggests a new insight or a new way of understanding a concept or explains a difficult concept well, expressing delight in this success and acknowledging the student's influence on your thinking can provide significant motivation for students. When a teacher communicates that the students can change the teacher's thinking or approach to teaching course material, the students are more likely to be motivated to engage in the kinds of behaviors likely to produce such insights.

Law teachers can show their confidence in themselves and their students by what they choose to teach, by the particular teaching methods they adopt, by the language they use as they teach, and by how they otherwise interact with their students. For example, the choice to teach difficult materials and to ask students to solve challenging problems manifests confidence in both the teacher and the students. The students get the idea that the teacher believes the students can learn anything.

Likewise, when teachers create learning activities in which students develop their own insights and must manifest their developing expertise, such as cooperative learning exercises, peer feedback experiences, and peer-to-peer teaching, they convey their belief that the students are capable. Well-designed cooperative learning experiences show faith in students because they allow students to negotiate meaning among themselves—the students construct ideas among themselves rather than passively receiving the ideas.

Very simple things, such as our body language in class, how we react to questions in class, how we deal with student frustration, and our comfort in demonstrating our expertise while acknowledging our errors also express our confidence. For example, respectfully listening to students, and finding and reinforcing the insights embedded in students' comments, course webpage contributions, and questions show that we are convinced that the students are perceptive and have promising futures in the field.

Authentic Experiences, Variety, and Active Learning

As we also explain in Chapters 1, 2, 4, and 6, students learn more and learn it better when they engage in a variety of authentic lawyering experiences that involve active learning. Authentic experiences, variety and active learning experiences also can be motivational because all three help maintain student interest in the learning process.

By situating students in their new roles as lawyers, authentic experiences explicitly connect students' new learning with their career aspirations. The concreteness of this link attracts students' interest. Students develop the motivation to learn because the connection between what they are learning and what they want to be doing is direct and the consequences of not learning seem more significant.

Variety and active learning experiences can be motivating because they capture students' attention and minimize distraction. Changes in the learning process recapture students' attention and motivate students to continue trying to learn, especially if the overall cycle of teaching methods includes techniques preferred by the students. Active learning motivates students because it prevents them from mentally withdrawing.

Structuring Student Autonomy

Student autonomy is highly correlated with student motivation. Thus, giving students power to make choices about how the class will be taught and what they will learn is particularly effective for motivating students. Disclosing learning goals, providing students with mechanisms to self-evaluate their progress, and explicitly explaining the criteria by which students will be evaluated (i.e., creating rubrics) also foster student autonomy. This information empowers students to control their own learning process.

Participation (Role-Playing)

Engaging students in role-plays can be particularly effective for motivating students. As explained above, asking students to assume their future lawyer role helps students identify the importance of what they are learning. But role-playing also can be useful for motivating students in other ways. Asking students to take the various roles involved in a transaction or dispute can motivate them to master difficult concepts by providing context with which they may not be familiar.

Challenge, Incongruity, and Conflict

Of all the techniques educators suggest as tools to motivate students to learn, incongruity and conflict is the one law professors most commonly use. The law school Socratic method focuses heavily on introducing students to considerations and ideas that either actually contradict their viewpoints or seem to do so. However, students cannot develop flow if they perceive success as unattainable. If you adopt this teaching method, make sure your students experience some success in resolving (or at least understanding) the conflicts and incongruities. Unending failure is de-motivating. Challenge works best as a motivational tool when the challenge is *both* reasonable and continuous. By sequencing course materials and learning activities so that the students' learning tasks are increasingly difficult, law teachers can make sure students get both the benefits of being challenged while also enjoying success and being reinforced for their persistence.

Reinforcement

Reinforcement also can be effective in motivating students. In general, however, reinforcement tends to focus students on extrinsic rather than intrinsic goals and therefore is less likely to persist as a motivator. Effective reinforcements include praise, public recognition, and unexpected prizes. Reinforcement also can take the form of eliminating an obstacle or hurdle that is unattractive to your students, such as allowing students to pass their way out of having to complete an exercise. In contrast, threats, surveillance practices, and punishments are less effective in stimulating motivation. These techniques tend to produce student anger, negativity and, in some instances, rebellion.

Teaching for Attitude or Value Change or Development

Law schools and teachers commonly assert that they want their students to develop the attitudes and values of professionalism, commitment to public service, sensitivity to diversity, respect for the rule of law, and belief in professional reflection and lifelong learning. The research suggests students can be taught values. As you might expect, however, simply telling students to have a value is seldom effective.

General Principles of Attitude Learning

Experts in attitude instruction focus on *evidence* of attitude change; that evidence is measured in terms of student behavior. Students have acquired a desired attitude if they consistently choose to engage in behaviors that express the desired attitude. For example, if the goal is to convince students to be self-regulated learners, students who, without being asked to do so, set mastery goals, reflect on their learning process, seek opportunities for practice and feedback, and adapt their learning approaches based on the task, the time available, and their past results, have acquired the desired attitude.

More specifically, attitude experts conceptualize changes in student attitudes along a wide spectrum as depicted in Illustration 5-1. At one end of the spectrum, the student merely engages in behavior that evidences the attitude. At the opposite end of the spectrum, the student has become so committed to the attitude that the student has become a role model or advocate for the behavior. In the middle of this spectrum are lesser degrees of dedication to the value, such as taking satisfaction when engaging in the behavior or committing to the behavior (choosing to engage in the behavior when no one else is watching).

It's also helpful to conceptualize attitude change in terms of three fundamental principles or elements: cognition, affect, and behavior. Cognition refers to knowing how to implement the new attitude. Affect refers to knowing why the behavior is valuable and therefore worthy of adoption. Behavior is implementing the attitude, especially if the person chooses to do so in the face of competing demands.

Illustration 5-1. Spectrum of Behavior Evidencing Attitude Change

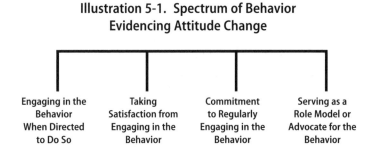

| Engaging in the Behavior When Directed to Do So | Taking Satisfaction from Engaging in the Behavior | Commitment to Regularly Engaging in the Behavior | Serving as a Role Model or Advocate for the Behavior |

Techniques for Producing Attitude Change

Three commonly-used techniques have been shown to influence attitudes: persuasion (trying to convince students to change by arguments and other messages), role modeling (using others to demonstrate the efficacy of adopting the attitude), and experience (creating an occurrence that juxtaposes the benefits of the desired attitude with students' existing attitudes). The discussion below considers each of these possibilities in the order of least to most effective. Persuasion is the least effective technique and, in fact, can be ineffective if the students are highly committed to their existing views. Experience is the most effective technique, especially if the experience positively juxtaposes the desired attitude against the students' previously held attitudes. Role modeling is somewhere in the middle in terms of its effectiveness.

Persuasion

Persuasion has two facets: the characteristics of the arguments and the source of the arguments. Effective arguments for change must be easy to understand, well-structured, and convincing, but the key to success is whether the arguments address a need or problem the students regard as personally significant. Because the students often do not perceive a need or problem, it is helpful to think of persuasion as needing to address two issues: (1) the existence of a need or problem, and (2) the advocated behavior that addresses the need or solves the problem. Finally, the research suggests that persuasion is most effective if the persuader explicitly articulates the attitude change for which he is arguing.

The source refers to the person who is making the argument (the speaker or the author of the argument). A source is most effective when it has one or both of two characteristics: credibility (expertise or education) and attractiveness (similarity to students or fame). The research recommends that teachers expressly establish the persuader's credibility. Accordingly, if you use a guest practitioner as a persuader, for example, make sure you tell the students about the speaker's expertise.

Upper-division students are commonly used for persuasion because of their similarity to the students. How many times have you had students adopt even crazy suggestions from an upper-division student (usually someone they bumped into in the student lunchroom) who claims to have done well in your class or to know "the secret" for doing well in your class? Using upper-division students allows you to undo some of the damage done by these lunchroom experts.

If you choose to use attractive persuaders, select a diverse group of persuaders and encourage them to open up with the students. A major factor in attractiveness is whether the students perceive that the persuader shares their attitudes with respect to issues other than those about which the persuader is speaking. By selecting a diverse group of persuaders and encouraging the persuaders to be open about themselves, their career goals, and their values, you increase the number of students who are likely to be influenced.

While persuasion can be effective and probably is the most commonly-used attitude-change technique, it typically only addresses the affective elements of attitude change. Persuaders only address why an attitude change is a good idea. Modeling adds in the cognitive element.

Modeling

In the context of law school, modeling refers to having a former student or a practitioner show the desired attitude and being rewarded for doing so. Credibility is as important for modeling as it is for persuasion. High credibility role models, people the students regard as worthy of imitation, are particularly effective. Effective role modeling enables students to observe the role model engaging in the behavior *and* observe the role model being reinforced for doing so. The combination of demonstration and observed reinforcement emphasizes the relationship between the two. For example, if students see a successful upper-division student engaging in self-regulated learning and witness the student being rewarded by good grades or exciting career opportunities, they are more likely to adopt the desired behavior. In this way, modeling addresses both the cognitive and the affective elements of attitude change.

Law professors have three potential sources of role models. First, you function as a role model, representing the profession to your students. For example, your professionalism and commitment in fulfilling your teaching role, communicates your values. Students quickly decide whether you are engaged, prepared, and committed. In addition, students notice whether you practice what you preach in terms of service to our communities, institutions, peers, and them.

Second, upper-division students are very convincing to other students. Accordingly, having upper-division students demonstrate, for example, their efforts at reflecting on the learning process, and then publically expressing your admiration for their efforts, can be effective in convincing students to become more reflective about their own studies. It would be hard, of course, for your upper-division students to model (during a class session) behaviors reflecting values such as professionalism and public service. The students may, instead, need to describe what they plan to do outside of class and, afterwards, report what they did.

Third, other practitioners make excellent role models. In particular, we suggest using former students who have become successful practitioners. For example, having an alumnus reflect on something he did in practice (take a deposition, argue a motion, try a case) and brainstorm how he will change his approach the next time he needs to perform a similar task may be an effective act of role modeling. Similarly, having a practitioner discuss her plans to do pro bono work and then report back on her experience can be effective. In this way, the practitioner helps students transfer the adoption of the value in law school to the form the value takes in law practice.

Role models are even more effective if the students try out the behavior themselves. Students who try out the new behaviors reflecting the desired value are likely to adopt that value because the activity both engages them and addresses the behavioral element of attitude change and development. Experience addresses all three elements.

Experience

Experience refers to students trying out the desired behavior and experiencing its benefits for themselves. Experiences are most effective if the conflict between the students' existing values and the desired value is readily identifiable and the students receive or discover the benefits from engaging in the alternative behavior. Because such experiences expose a discrepancy between the students' existing values and the desired value, many educational researchers use the term "dissonance" to refer to this strategy.

The challenge is to design experiences that are authentic, give students as much autonomy in the process as possible, and allow students to experience the benefits of adopting the desired value. An experience is authentic if the students are engaging in the behavior in a way that is as similar to how they might act in the future. For example, using actual course feedback (e.g., a grade on a paper, comments on a practice exam) as a springboard for getting students to engage in self-regulation increases the likelihood students will make the connection between the self-regulation activity and their other efforts at learning. An experience gives students autonomy if the students have some choice in the process. For example, asking students to engage in public service but to choose for themselves the particular form of public service gives students autonomy and increases the likelihood that they will value the experience they have chosen. If the students do not experience any reward from adopting the behavior, experience is unlikely to change their attitudes. On the other hand, if, for example, the students get a sense they are learning more by reflecting on their learning process, they are more likely to adopt this behavior as their own. Such natural rewards, rewards inherent in adopting the desired attitude, are more effective than grades or other extrinsic rewards because the natural rewards develop student's intrinsic interest in adopting the behavior.

Experience can address all there elements of behavioral change. Experience addresses the behavioral element of attitude change because the students are actually implementing the desired behavior.

Experience also addresses the cognitive element because the students are trying out the techniques for themselves and can receive coaching in their efforts at implementation. Experience may most effectively address the affective element of change because, rather than being told about the benefits or seeing someone else get the benefits from implementing the desired behavior, the students actually experience the benefits for themselves.

Checklist for Teaching for Motivation and Attitude Change

Illustration 5-2 is a checklist for teaching for motivation and attitude change. This checklist summarizes things law professors can do to better motivate students.

Illustration 5-2. Teaching for Motivation and Attitude Change Checklist

❏   Adopt attitudinal strategies
 ❏   Passion and enthusiasm
 ❏   Confidence
❏   Create authentic lawyering experiences
❏   Use variety of teaching techniques
❏   Structure opportunities for student autonomy
❏   Encourage student goal-setting
❏   Create non-threatening challenge, incongruity, and conflict to spark interest
❏   Provide reinforcement
❏   Find optimal role models
❏   Make sure students try out both the desired behavior and receive rewards for engaging in it

You will find examples of the concepts from this chapter in Appendix 8 on the book's website—http://lawteaching.org/resources/books/teachinglawbydesign/teachinglawbydesign-appendices.pdf.

Appendix 5-1: Role Plays

Appendix 5-2: Experiential Professionalism Instruction

Appendix 5-3: Time Management/Self-Monitoring Log

Appendix 5-4: Post-Assessment Reflection Exercises

Chapter 6

Teaching the Class

This chapter focuses on the nuts and bolts of "live" teaching—when you and the students are all physically present in one location. Bear in mind that there is no single way to teach the class effectively; the goal is to have effective classes for most students most of the time.

Keep one fundamental question in mind as you teach your class:

"Who in the room is acting like a lawyer?"

Keeping this question paramount in your mind as you teach will help you focus on your learning goals and maximize students' experience. The more the students are *engaged in acting like lawyers—speaking and doing—the more they are likely to learn.*

A related question about live teaching is,

"Who is doing most of the talking in class?"

Conventional teaching focuses on *what the teachers do* in the classroom—what the teacher says and how the teacher presents information or questions. To enhance student learning, focus on a different image: *Teaching is creating a place in which students learn.* Creating a place in which students learn means that your role in the classroom is **less** about what you say and **more about what students are doing.** In the classroom, try to ensure that most students are acting like lawyers as they engage in applying the learning objectives you have identified. This chapter suggests ways to make this happen.

Create a Positive Learning Environment Where Students Feel That It Is Safe to Take Risks

Before considering teaching "nuts and bolts" techniques, consider the "art" side of live teaching, the "feel" of the class. Creating a positive learning environment is critical to student learning and takes more than teaching technique and subject matter expertise. Below are some suggestions about what you can do to help build a positive classroom environment.

Know and Use Students' Names

If you have a hard time learning names, practice with flash cards. If learning students' names quickly is not feasible, we recommend that you use name cards (see Illustration 6-1) so that you can regularly use students' names during the class.

Practice students' names outside of class — a few minutes a day. Regular practice, a commitment to learning students' names, and using name cards enables most teachers to learn students' names within a few weeks, even in classes of over 100 students.

Be Conscious of the Messages You Send

Communication experts tell us that 75% of our message is delivered by body language. When in the classroom, be aware of what your body language may convey to students. Eye contact, listening attentively, and projecting a sense of confidence and openness are as important as any specific technique.

Find a way to see students positively. You may think of them as friends you have invited to a dinner party, offspring, or young relatives (how would I respond if my favorite niece asked that question?) Consider them future colleagues in practice or on the bench. Whatever you do, find something to be positive about.

Illustration 6-1. Name Cards

Using Name Cards

In classes of more than twenty, we find it helpful to have students bring "table tents" or "UN Name Cards" to class. These name cards have students' names printed in large font on the front and back. With the names on both sides, students can learn each others' names.

These cards are printed on heavy card stock paper so that they stand up and last for at least a few weeks. A faculty administrative assistant can print these off your rosters. On the first day of class, you distribute the name cards and make a heavy black marker available to those who want to be called by a different name.

Alternatively you can bring in photocopy paper, ask students to fold in half lengthwise and write their names in ALL CAPS on both sides, using a heavy black marker.

Encourage students to bring the name cards to class until you know all their names — even better, wait until all students know each others' names. (Sophie asks students to put the name cards in a book they regularly bring to class or tape to the back of their laptop so that they always have them with them.) The table tents help you and the students attach names to faces starting on the first day of class.

Be Enthusiastic

Students greatly appreciate it when you project confidence and enthusiasm, and you can always find something to be enthusiastic about. Show enthusiasm with small gestures: start the class with a smile and "Good evening!" Students enjoy learning from teachers who clearly like students and teaching.

Model Taking Risks and Acknowledging Weaknesses

Students respect and appreciate teachers who are self-confident and acknowledge their weaknesses. It's ok to say, "Great question. I never thought of that. I'll have to think about it and get back to you." If you are trying something new, tell students something like, "I'm going out on a limb here. I am not sure if this exercise will work, but I am going to ask you to engage in a different kind of learning activity today."

When you make a mistake (we've all made tons), acknowledge it. "Last class I gave you some misinformation. Let me try to clarify." Let them know that you, too, have to work at writing complex prose, speaking in public, and teaching effectively. Apologize when you err. Admitting your errors and asking for students' pardon treats students with respect.

Be Transparent and Authentic

Explain to students what you are doing and why. Even if students want a concrete answer to an unresolved issue, explain why the answer is "it depends" and what it depends on. When you use different instructional activities, explain why, at least the first few times you use them. Be honest and direct. You may say that there is no right answer, but you mean there is no *one* single right answer. Instead there is a cluster of right answers and a group of wrong ones.

As the educator Parker Palmer says, "We teach who we are." If your style is to be self-deprecating and you are good at telling jokes, do so. Don't try to be someone you are not. It often takes several years of teaching to develop your teaching persona. Pay attention and be patient.

The Nuts and Bolts

This part of the chapter has four main sections:

- Pre-class—the fifteen minutes before class starts
- Openings—the first five minutes
- Body—the heart of the class session
  - Instructional activities
  - Lectures
  - Questioning techniques
  - Addressing controversial issues
  - Visuals
  - Discovery sequence instruction
  - Timing
- Closings—the last five minutes

In class, tell students what you want them to learn (opening of class), engage them in instructional exercises to help them learn (body), and summarize what you wanted them to learn (closing).

Pre-Class: The 15 Minutes before Class Starts— Arrive Early

Showing up at least 15 minutes before class allows you to take care of any problems and shows that you are interested in the students. For the first class, figure out how you plan to use the room. Practice using the technology, including chalk or markers. Make sure everyone will have a seat and can see the board or screen. If all systems are working, use the time to set out materials, project first slides, or write your objectives on the board. In the remaining time, chat with the early students, take a deep breath, or focus on your learning goals.

Openings: The First Five Minutes of Class — Provide an Overview

The beginning of class sets the tone and prepares your students to learn. Make a positive first impression — show students your enthusiasm, confidence and respect. Some specific suggestions:

Provide Students with the Objectives at the Beginning of Class

Give students the "road map" of the class. Using two ways of providing information, such as visually and verbally, makes it more likely students will retain it. Visually show the class learning goals on a slide, a handout, or on the board. Verbally flesh out the objectives and provide the context of the class in the learning unit and the course. For example you could say:

> *In the last few classes we analyzed a range of crimes, ending with murder. We looked at what a prosecutor would need to prove to charge a defendant with negligent homicide, manslaughter, felony murder, and first- and second-degree murder. In groups you made arguments applying the elements of those felonies to different factual situations.*
>
> *Today we are moving to conspiracy. Specifically, today we are investigating prosecution and defendant arguments for conspiracy and attempted conspiracy. We will be building upon the same skills — articulating the law, facts and policy — in making and responding to arguments.*

You can further explain what will be happening in the body of the class:

> *Today you will be working with one partner to compare and analyze your individual responses to Problem 7-A, using cases A, B, and C.*

See If Students Have Any Questions Arising from the Previous Class Sessions

After you've asked if students have any questions, pause and mentally count to five to allow students a chance to gather their thoughts. If you don't want to respond to any questions, don't ask. If students have many questions, answer a few of them and then move on, encouraging students to email you, talk to you after class, or post questions or comments on a course webpage.

Administrative Matters

Find out what your institution requires for tracking attendance, and take attendance at the beginning of class. One of the easiest ways to do this is to circulate a list of the enrolled students next to which students can sign their names.

Modifications — First Day of the Course; Other Significant Classes

The First Day of the Course

The first day of the course is special. Your opening may be longer, giving you time to tell a story about the course, practice, or yourself.

Explain any policies for attendance, seating and using names. Some teachers like to be called "Professor X," others are comfortable with a range of names. You can say:

> *My name is Pat Davis. You can call me Pat, Ms. Davis or Professor Davis. I will call you by whatever name you prefer. Today I will go through the roster; let me know if I have mispronounced your name or if you have a different name you would like to use.*

Explain your views on teaching and ask for students' help:

We'll be using a variety of teaching and learning strategies in this class. I will lecture, ask you to do group work, in-class exercises, and practice other lawyering skills. You all have different learning preferences and not all techniques may be ideal for you. I ask for your forbearance when we are using a style that works for others, but not for you.

When Students Face Crises or Distractions

Delay the formal opening to allow a time for reflection, silence, and a chance to discuss. Whether a student has become severely ill or lost a family member, or a catastrophe has hit the area, acknowledge the crisis and give students some quiet time.

As most of you may have heard, last night terrible storms attacked the west coast. I know that many of you have been concerned about family and friends who were in the area and whom you have had a hard time contacting. Let's take five minutes to sit in silence or write. At the end of that time, anyone who wants to can share thoughts about this tragedy.

If this isn't your style, you might just want to acknowledge the event and move on. Be authentic and remember that students crave to connect with our humanity.

I heard about the shooting in City X yesterday and am very sorry for all those involved. If any of you would like to talk to me about it outside of class, I would be happy to do so.

Similarly, acknowledge challenges facing students. Many students become stressed and tired in November and March as they face final exam pressure. Acknowledge that stress and invite them to focus on the class.

OK, so many of you are preoccupied. For now, I am going to ask you to set those concerns aside for the next 40 minutes and practice being securities lawyers.

Body — The Heart of the Class Session

The body of a class session is where you will be spending the most time, focusing on what you want students to learn by the end of the class. The body of the class is the total class time minus about ten minutes (five minutes for the opening and five for the closing.) Keep your class outline and learning objectives present on a handout, slide or board; this will make you less likely to try to cover too much material or go off on tangents.

Focus on One to Three Learning Objectives per One-Hour Class Session

Once you have identified the learning objectives for each class (Chapter 4), work backwards to design effective class sessions. For example, if you want students to outline the steps involved in registering a new trademark, identify what they need to do and how you will know whether they have correctly outlined the steps. Sketch out how much time you want to have students work on each class objective. Remember that they are more likely to retain a deep understanding of this process if they are actively engaged.

Instructional Activities

Use instructional activities that engage students, helping them practice acting like lawyers.

Students are engaged when they are:

- Writing
- Talking and listening
- Reading
- Reflecting

Illustration 6-2 lists five active learning instructional activities you can use in the body of your class. Each of these activities is described briefly below. When they are engaged in these activities, the students, and not just the teacher, are "doing the work" — practicing acting like lawyers. They are actively solving problems, thinking, talking, listening, taking notes, reading, and writing. When you use these techniques, watch the energy, volume, and activity in the class soar.

You don't need to be an expert in these activities to be an effective teacher. Many simple, quick techniques can be included in law school classes. Start simple, start small, and give yourself time to work these into your classes and learn from experiences. For each class, remember to ask yourself, "Who in this room is acting like a lawyer?" *and* "Who in this room is talking?" *Choose one or two new instructional activities a semester. Don't give up just because they didn't work as well as you hoped the first time or some students didn't like them.*

Ideally, use three or more different instructional activities per class. Variety keeps the class interesting, engages students in different levels of thinking, and addresses different learning preferences. Consider Socratic-style questioning as one kind of instructional activity (more on Socratic-style questioning below) and mix it with other instructional activities.

Illustration 6-2. Instructional Activities: Active Learning Selections

- Think-write-pair-share
- Small group discussion
- Student-to-student group discussion
- Small group role-playing
- Point/counterpoint

Think-Write-Pair-Share

This technique is one of the quickest, easiest, and most versatile activities. Pose a question verbally or in writing. Ask students to think about the question for a minute and then jot down a response. Once they have completed their responses (one-to-three minutes depending on the question's complexity) ask students to exchange their ideas with a neighbor. Ask them to discuss their answers and the reasons for them (one-three minutes).

Call on a few students to provide responses, or ask one or two students to volunteer his or her neighbor's response. Note responses on the board, enter and project them on a screen, or verbally reinforce responses. After students have talked with a neighbor, who has either acknowledged confusion with the issue, or affirmed the student's response, a much greater range of students volunteer and are comfortable being called on.

Small-Group Discussion

Pose a question or problem that students must work together to solve. Students can collectively discuss and answer questions at different levels of thinking, e.g., What are the elements of the statute? Which element is at issue in this client's case? How would you describe federal preemption to a lay person?

As the groups work, you may decide to circulate among them, be available as a resource for students to call upon, sit in and listen to a few groups, or allow them to work on their own. If you circulate, you can identify and address any common areas of confusion and get a sense of how the groups are functioning. If you allow the groups to work on their own, at least some of your students may be more likely to take risks. Once groups have discussed their responses, call on a couple of different students—ideally those who have previously not contributed to the large group discussion—to talk about the group's responses. Once you have a response, invite students who had a different response to contribute.

A word about using small groups effectively. Small group assignments must have crystal clear directions. Specify an amount of time for students to work in groups. Allow less time than you think students will need, and add time if students are still focused and more time would help them attain the learning goals. You can gauge how things are going by asking the class as a whole or circulating and asking different groups whether they would like another couple of minutes. If all the groups are working on the same problem, avoid having groups do a "reporting back" where each group gives a presentation on the same topic. (The reporting back group responses get tiresome and most students disengage after a few minutes.)

Student-to-Student Group Discussion

Ask the students to lead the discussion by calling on each other. For example, after posing a question about a rule, factual analysis or other teaching objective, explain to students that the goal of the next few minutes is for them to achieve that objective by talking to and calling on each other without your involvement. You can start the discussion by asking a student, perhaps one who has previously not spoken, to respond to the question you have posed. After she or he has contributed, each subsequent student must call on the next one to further the discussion. While students talk and refine their understanding, you or another student can serve as scribe and note responses on the board.

Small Group Role-Playing and Simulations

Divide the class in sections, and assign a role to each. For example, in an employment law class, you might assign one group to the role of employees, one to employers, one to in-house counsel, and one to legislators. In small groups, ask the students to collectively outline the large-scale structure of their positions, using notes or bullet points. Tell them to think about the big picture, not get stuck on the particular words or polished language and note that they may want to start in the middle or end and bounce around as they work through the outline. One or two groups from each section could write their outline on chart paper, overheads, board or laptop, and then show the analysis to the whole class.

Point/Counterpoint

Divide the class in half, with half the students representing one party and half the another, and ask students to take turns making their arguments. In this portion of the session, ask a participant on one side of the room to make one statement in support of an argument, and then identify someone on the opposite side of the room who will make a statement either refuting the argument or making a different argument supporting the opposite outcome. Continue for a few minutes as both sides of the room explore the analysis. At the end of this portion, ask students to raise their hands to identify, given the materials they have, what the strongest arguments are. You can also do this exercise with a small prop, such as a squishy ball or soft toy that students toss back and forth across the room. Emphasize that the idea is to toss gently to another student, rather than demonstrate throwing prowess.

Additional Points about Instructional Activities

Keep Track of the Time

Active learning instructional activities can take on a life of their own. Help keep students on task and focused on the learning objectives. If individual or groups of students finish an activity early, have additional instructional activities they can engage in.

Close the Loop

After students have engaged in learning activities, explain what they have done and reinforce the learning you have observed. You can summarize main points, invite students to share what they learned, or clarify students' questions.

Sometimes it is hard to reconvene the class as a whole once students have engaged in active learning. Techniques to reconvene class include briefly turning on and off the lights, calling students' attention to the class, giving students a warning about how many minutes they have left, and using their names "I see that Carlos's and Kim's groups are ready to discuss their responses with the class.... Others?"

Lectures

Lectures can lead to significant student learning. They are most effective when they are:

- Short (10–15 minutes max)
- Add valuable content
- Surrounded by other activities
- Supported by visuals
- Delivered effectively

Use Mini-Lectures — 10 to 15 Minutes

Studies show that, within ten minutes, students' attention considerably drops off. No matter how dynamic we are as speakers, few people retain more than a small portion of a lecture. Mini-lectures are highly effective in addressing students' misconceptions about a concept, giving feedback to students, or summarizing a portion of the class. Mini-lectures are most effective when you give them *after* students have done some preparation and engaged in problem solving. Then students are primed to pay attention; they realize where they need guidance.

Add Valuable Content

Don't include in a lecture anything you can put in print unless doing so will likely help students learn. Instead, build upon what you have assigned students to prepare, or highlight important points that were not in written material or may need emphasis.

Surround Mini-Lectures with Other Activities

Sandwich mini-lectures between a small group discussion, active learning technique, or other activities that engage your students. Include pauses between main points to allow students to catch up on notes, review, and consolidate their thinking.

Include Visuals

Use pictures, graphics, props and other material — widely available on the internet — to reinforce important points. Consider giving students a barebones outline or chart into which they can take notes; the mental effort students use to complete the outline helps hold their attention.

Deliver Mini-Lectures Effectively

Use a voice audible from the back of the room. Vary your phrasing and allow for pauses. Avoid speaking in a monotone. Move around. Make eye contact with students. Periodically include students' names, "So if Marcella was filing a patent claim, she would ..." Tell students which points are especially important and encourage them to write them down. Repeat main points during the mini-lecture to reorient novice learners.

Questioning Techniques

Using questions or engaging in "Socratic" dialogue can be one of the most effective ways to engage students in achieving all levels of critical thinking. One of the greatest weaknesses of traditional law school Socratic-style discussion is that most students are not engaged. Certainly, the selected student is actively engaged in the one-on-one conversation with the teacher and receives feedback on her learning process. For all the other students in the class the learning process is vicarious at best. Some students are shopping electronically, e-mailing other professors, or sending each other messages unrelated to class. Ways to make Socratic-style questioning effective and engaging:

- Prepare students in advance
- Ask clear questions, one at a time
- Ask a range of questions
- Allow sufficient wait-time (three seconds or more)
- Encourage effective responses and respond appropriately to ineffective answers

Prepare Students in Advance

From handouts, web pages, syllabi, or other formats, give students enough information in advance so that they are prepared to discuss the questions. (See Chapters 3, 4, and 5.) For more complex thinking skills, giving students core questions in advance will help them target their out-of-class studying.

Model the kinds of responses you want. For example, present students with a problem and then model how you would solve the problem, talking through each step, and admitting where you are stumped in the process. Pause as you go, allowing students to catch up with you and take notes.

Ask Clear Questions

Write down the questions in advance to ensure they align with your class learning objectives. For students who are not auditory learners, or speak English as a second language, projecting your questions on a PowerPoint slide or writing on the board will allow the students to more readily process the question. If you have a definite point you want a student to make, state a proposition and ask students whether and why they agree or disagree.

Help students by naming what you want them learn, such as by asking, "The court used a number of factors in rejecting the claim for punitive damages. I'm wondering if you all identified the same factors, or interpreted this opinion differently. Phil, please start us off by identifying one of the factors that the court seems to use." If you don't wish to call on a particular student, invite any student to respond, "Could someone start ...?"

Ask One Question at a Time

If you see students' blank looks after asking a question, resist throwing out other questions, or tacking on additional points. Discipline yourself to staying with one question at a time. Repeat a question if it is long or complex, but don't add questions as it will compound student confusion. Writing questions out in advance helps avoiding such problems.

Ask a Range of Questions

Open-ended questions are more likely to generate discussion than yes/no questions. Vary the kind of question and the length of time it takes students to respond. As you progress through the course, ask students questions at increasingly more complex levels. Embed material about a concept studied earlier in a question about the current class topic, for example: "Let's review the tests administrative agencies use to ... [name tests briefly]. Let's apply those factors to ..."

Allow Sufficient Wait-Time (at Least Three to Five Seconds) after You Ask a Question

Most of us struggle with silence in the classroom. The research shows that we usually wait only a second or two before we fill the silence by making a comment or rephrasing the question. One second is not enough time for most students to generate a meaningful response. Giving yourselves and students time to process the question usually results in more students being able to answer your question. You can explain this fact to students to address the awkwardness of the quiet. "I am going to wait for 5 seconds to give you time to think," or, "I see that Ee Ming, and Rafael have answers to this question. How about some others? I'll wait."

Another way to provide students with time to process the question is to ask them to write a response in 30 seconds or to engage in a think-write-pair-share exercise as described above. These processes allow students a chance to reflect and work through their thinking for a particular response.

Encourage and Promote Effective Responses, Respond Appropriately to Ineffective Answers

When a students responds to a questions, stop moving and look at the student, leaning slightly toward him or her. Acknowledge students' effective responses, both when they respond and later, e.g., "Remember Louisa's excellent point about …" Invite students to develop their responses. "Great start! Now can you help me out by explaining how you arrived at that answer?" Smile, nod, be quiet, and make eye contact to help students elaborate their response. Write students' responses on the board, and invite others to help their classmates to build student confidence in responding to questions. Acknowledge students' insights that are new to you; your students will appreciate your respect for them and your self-confidence in your expertise.

When students give a "wrong" answer, guide them to a better response, if at all possible. Focus on the answer, not on the student, and acknowledge any positive aspect of the response. Using a gentle sense of humor can also help diffuse a potentially uncomfortable moment for the student, "Oh, good, that is so-o-o close! But I am wondering if that answer might be missing something. How about taking a look further down the page where it says …" Try hints (e.g., "Why do you think the court mentioned _____ fact?") or cues (e.g., "Is there anything in the federal rules that you might use as a basis for support in making your argument?"). You can also invite the student to ask for "co-counsel" to assist, and then return to the student to have the student end the discussion with a positive contribution.

Discovery Sequence Instruction

Discovery sequence instruction involves providing students a series of examples and non-examples of a concept and labeling each as either an example or non-example and then asking students to infer the principle or principles that reconcile the examples and non-examples. For example, provide students a set of examples and non-examples of contracts to which Article II of the UCC would apply or of activities for which a person successfully could be charged with conspiracy and then ask students to infer the principles. You could also provide students with a set of effective and ineffective responses to a hypothetical and ask the students to explain the principles that distinguish the effective responses.

Using Real-Life Experiences

Another powerful instructional technique is bringing real life scenarios into the course. Bringing real life into the course can be done in a wide variety of ways, including:

- Photos
- Videos
- News stories
- Documents (contracts, pleadings, tax returns)
- Interviews of practicing lawyers and judges
- Field trips (court, agency, business)
- Service learning experiences (domestic violence shelter, low income tax advice)
- Research papers applying the course to real-life).

Real-life examples or experiences allow students to see abstract concepts concretely. For example, a photo of a nuclear waste facility located next to a river may have a powerful effect on students' understanding of environmental law. Inviting students to research current issues and events, and having students follow new legislation or community issues also involves students in applying their classroom learning to practice.

Using Simulations to Promote Deep Learning

Simulations are particularly effective for some students; students who struggle with learning through verbal discussion and reading and writing often excel when they are asked to simulate the role of an attorney. Some simulations engage students in comprehensive and complex scenarios the whole semester. Others engage students for a shorter period, such as drafting and negotiating a contract, making a presentation for a simulated client, or conducting a mock client interview. Computer-assisted learning also can provide students with ways to practice solving the kinds of problems lawyers face.

Address Controversial Issues

Sensitive issues or challenging behaviors arise in almost every course. According to students, one of the worst things we can do as teachers is to ignore these sensitive issues of race, class, politics, religion, gender, and sexual orientation. Instead, we can acknowledge the challenge and invite students to engage in a respectful discussion about the topic.

When facing challenging issues, students need to see us model calm and constructive leadership. Think of yourself as someone responding to a 911 call. The first rule is to stay calm. Take a deep breath. Try to disengage for a minute and consider the view of the classroom dynamic from above the class. What just happened? Why might a student have reacted that way? We can name the challenge, use silence, and ask students to pause and reflect on what just happened in the classroom. "I see that many of you are uncomfortable with the opinion just stated, that health insurance should never cover the cost of an abortion. Before we continue, let's pause for a minute to think about why some of us might hold that view." We want students' to learn how to listen to controversial views and to try to understand others' perspectives.

Depending on the class, you may also want to delay the conversation for the next class.

> An important issue has just come up in class. We don't have enough time to do justice to this right now, so I would like you all to think about this issue. We will talk about this issue in the next class. I invite everyone who would like to stay after class to talk about this issue to come talk to me. I am also more than happy to talk to you about this during office hours, via e-mail, or on the course webpage.

This approach allows you and your students time to reflect, shows that you are not avoiding the issue, and provides a definite time when the issue will be addressed. Only take this approach if you will actually deliver on your promise.

Allow students to discuss hot topics in class, but don't allow students to be personally attacked. If a student says something pejorative, such as, "Anyone who believes that praying in public school is OK is an idiot," rephrase the comment to make it one for general discussion, such as stating, "In fact, many smart, thoughtful people believe that there is a place for praying and spirituality in public education. Why might they think so?"

With any hot topic, it is often very helpful to talk to students after class. It is hard enough to discuss controversial issues with a small group of acquaintances; having an audience of 20 to 100 is even more difficult. Trying to understand individual students' experiences, reactions and suggestions for how they can learn from the experience may often be best done outside the class. If a student becomes very upset in class, we urge you to talk to the student outside of class. If unavailable right after class, we suggest you email the student noting that you were aware that the student was involved in a controversial discussion and encouraging him to talk to you about it in person. In some cases, such as where a student is extremely upset, you may want to contact your administration or dean of students to find out what other steps you can or should take.

Visuals

In this section we address a couple of visual attributes of the classroom, including PowerPoint and dress.

PowerPoint and Other Visuals

To include visuals that will help students learn, keep in mind a few essentials. For any visual device, whether a computer projection, movie clip, or black or white board, the key is whether all students can "read" the visual. Check out the sight lines from all points in the room. Less is more. Use bigger letters, numbers, and images. Have fewer of them.

When projecting text, apply principles of effective graphics:

- Use text boxes, bullets, white space, numbered lists, and color.
- Use a font without feet like Arial—these are easier to read when enlarged.
- Limit text to six lines of type or less, which increases the likelihood your students can read your text.
- Limit the text to the important points. Include additional points on another slide, or amplify the material verbally.
- Unless there is a good reason for doing so, when you are in the classroom, don't look at the projected text and read it.

Instead, face the students, use the text as a focal point, and then engage students in discussion.

If you are using any kind of a projected image, practice the technology in advance and be prepared to have an alternate plan when the technology fails.

A final thought about using PowerPoint. It is tempting to use PowerPoint slides solely to transmit information—e.g., the language of a statute, three points you want to make in a lecture. If you only transmit knowledge using PowerPoint, however, your students may conclude that your course is mostly or exclusively about acquiring knowledge. By including questions, problems, visual metaphors, or even a checklist that addresses the process of using a skill you are teaching, you communicate a much different message about what's important in your class.

Dress

Dress is an issue for all teachers. For teachers who don't fit the traditional profile of a law professor, dress is especially important. Some suggestions:

There Is No One Right Way to Dress

What you choose to wear to the classroom will depend on your personality, your institution, your comfort level, and your students.

Consider the Dress Culture at Your Institution

If you have questions, talk to your colleagues about these unspoken norms. If you want ideas about how your students might perceive teachers your age, look at media images of people in authority.

Wear Comfortable Clothing That Makes You Feel Confident

Putting on a suit can create confidence: "Even if I am scared out of my wits, I'll at least look the part of a law professor." Some women feel most confident wearing pants; others feel they project a desired image of professionalism when they wear skirts. Similarly, some men feel better wearing a jacket; others feel confident so long as they wear a collared shirt and tie *or* jacket but don't feel a need for both. Whatever you decide to wear, try it out before you wear it in the classroom.

Adjust Your Clothing during the Semester, If Appropriate

Most of us are more formal at the beginning of the semester, when we want to make the best first impression with our students. As the semester continues, and students start to show stress, you may want to adopt more casual attire. One teacher pulls out his cardigan sweaters for those days.

Timing

Map out and prioritize chunks of time along with your learning objectives. For example, you might divide a 50-minute class into three sections of 13 minutes each, leaving 10 minutes for the opening and closing of the class session. Rather than setting the exact timing for each instructional activity, consider what you want students to have been doing for each 13-minute chunk of time. **Remember, you want students to be the ones acting like lawyers in the class.**

Many of us worry that we have enough material to "fill the time." If you are focusing on **what the students are doing**, you will wonder instead how you can help students learn sophisticated skills within the body of class.

For example, you have 40 minutes for the body of class. You plan the following:

- Small group discussion: 7 minutes
- Whole class discussion: 6 minutes
- Mini-lecture summarizing and clarifying: 10 minutes
- Think-Write-Pair-Share: 3 minutes
- Whole class discussion: 14 minutes

In the classroom, however, you find that students need more time in the small group discussions. Because students seem engaged and on task, you extend the time to ten minutes. If you get behind, go back to your learning objectives. What is it that students should learn by the end of this class? Of the instructional activities you have planned, which one is most likely to help students achieve those learning objectives in the time left? Rather than cramming all the instructional activities into the remaining time, scrap one or more of those activities and focus on the one that you think will be most effective. If you plan for this in advance, you can determine which instructional activities you definitely want students to engage in, and which ones are not essential, but would be lovely to use if time allows.

Respect the majority of the students by focusing the discussion on what students should be learning in class. One technique to help keep students on task and limit discussion is saying something like, "Last comment goes to Jo," even when three other people have their hands in the air. Another is stating, "Let's hear two more contributions. I'd like to hear from students who have not yet contributed to the class discussion." If you have decided not to call on volunteers who are the most frequent contributors, talk to them outside of class, letting them know that you appreciate their eagerness and enthusiasm, and that you want to be sure a variety of students' voices are heard in class.

If you have extra time in class, return to your learning objectives. Because being able to articulate ideas in writing is such an important lawyering skill, even if students are "done" with the discussion, ask students to prepare an outline summarizing key points. When students have to move beyond talking to writing and organizing, they frequently identify gaps in their analysis. Another solution is to prepare an "extra" instructional activity that you use during the class if you have time.

It is hard to know how the class will go. Spend time before class rehearsing, refining and tracking how long it takes. No matter what else you do, **end the class on time.** Track time so that you leave five minutes at the end for the closing.

Closings:
The Last Five Minutes of Class

Use the last five minutes of class to consolidate students' learning, mirroring the opening. Three examples are below.

Summarize Key Points

In the last few minutes of class, summarize the key learning points by using a skeletal outline on the board or a slide and verbally adding to it. (This may be the same outline or slide that you used at the beginning of class.)

> *Today you focused on the skill of identifying ambiguity in contracts. You noticed ambiguities in the words used, such as "damage to property or physical injury." The phrase was ambiguous because "damage" alone included physical and economic damage. You also noticed ambiguities created by ...* [continues]
> *You noticed ambiguities I hadn't seen and other classes hadn't seen. You learned that, while this effort may seem picky in a class, it can cost a party millions of dollars. You've discussed what steps you could take as lawyers to identify ambiguity in drafting contracts.*
> *You've worked through all but the final, most complex problem. Please review that for next class; we'll start with that problem and then move on to the next topic....*
> *Thank you and see you Monday.*

Give Students Time to Consolidate Their Learning

Involve the students in reflecting and consolidating the class objectives.

Today you had evaluated different proposed temporary restraining orders. In your groups, you saw five examples of how these might be drafted, and evaluated the effectiveness of different versions. Now I'd like you to take a minute to write a few notes to yourself. If in practice or on an exam you needed to draft a proposed temporary restraining order, what important things would you want to remind yourself to do?

Allow students a few minutes to write. Then ask students to compare their notes with someone else, or invite the class as a whole to contribute a few important points.

Allow Students to Reflect on Their Learning

This closing lets students practice the skills they need to become independent learners.

Today, you were assigned to play the roles of constituents seeking to resolve a toxic landfill problem. Some of you represented the landowner, others the neighbors, the city, legislators, the company that produced the toxins, and consumers who would benefit from the toxins. Think about and then write down one thing you learned from this exercise.

As with the previous suggestion, you could then invite students to compare their notes with each other, share with the whole class, or thank the students for participating and let them leave when they have finished writing.

Closing Modification: The Very Last Class — Leave Ten to Fifteen Minutes for the Final Closing

The last class, like the first class, is special. Some teachers like to summarize the course, talking about what the students have learned, thanking students for their efforts, and revealing what the teacher most appreciated about sharing the learning with this group of students. Other teachers use the last class as a chance to build students' confidence. They may tell students about the mistakes they made in their lives, and give ideas about how to navigate the stress of final exams. They may tell stories about practice and life. They may offer their assistance and support for future years. They may ask a final question. One of our colleagues stands at the door and shakes the hand of each exiting student. Like any other aspect of teaching, be authentic. Do something you enjoy doing, and try different approaches to ending the course.

Final Notes on Teaching the Class

All teachers have good days and bad days. Don't seek "perfection." You are the single most expensive, most adaptive, most empathic educational resource available to your students to learn what they need to learn in your course. Consider the small steps you can take to help students act as lawyers in the classroom. Reflect and learn from the experience.

Checklist for Teaching the Class

Illustration 6-3 is a checklist you can use for teaching the class.

Illustration 6-3. Teaching the Class Checklist

❏ **Consider:**

❏ **Who in the room is acting like a lawyer?**

❏ **Who is doing most of the talking in the class?**

   ❏ **Create a positive learning environment**
- ❏ Know and use students' names
- ❏ Be conscious of the messages you send
- ❏ Be enthusiastic
- ❏ Model taking risks and acknowledging weaknesses
- ❏ Envision yourself as a "guide on the side"
- ❏ Be transparent
- ❏ Be authentic

   ❏ **Openings — the first five minutes**
- ❏ Arrive early
- ❏ Consider the opening message you send
- ❏ Modify for first and other special days

   ❏ **Body — the heart of the class session**
- ❏ Use a variety of instructional activities
- ❏ Use activities that engage the students
- ❏ Use mini-lectures surrounded by other activities
- ❏ Use effective questioning techniques
- ❏ Address controversial issues
- ❏ Use visuals students can "read"
- ❏ Prioritize you timing according to learning objectives

   ❏ **Closings — the last five minutes**
- ❏ Summarize and consolidate students' learning
- ❏ Modify for the last class

   ❏ **Engage in ongoing practice, reflection and evaluation**

You will find examples of the concepts from this chapter in Appendix 6 on the book's website—http://lawteaching.org/resources/books/teachinglawbydesign/teachinglawbydesign-appendices.pdf.

Appendix 6-1: Discovery Sequence Exercises
     Duty to Disclose Discovery Sequence Exercise
     Binding vs. Persuasive Authority Discovery Sequence
     Exercise

Chapter 7

Assessing Student Learning

Introduction

In this chapter, we focus on designing effective assessment approaches and instruments, both to give you and the students feedback during the course and to assign grades.

Illustration 7-1 identifies the steps essential to any assessment process.

Illustration 7-1. Designing Effective Assessments — 3 Steps

1. Identify what you want to assess (learning objectives)
2. Prepare and give assessment instruments
3. Give feedback to students

Step One: Identify Learning Objectives

Learning objectives should articulate the knowledge, skills, and values you expect students to learn in the course. If you are unsure about your learning objectives, consider what you expect students to do well in the course. The kinds of intellectual skills and knowledge you test on the final exam are good indicators of what you want students to learn in the course. For further guidance, look at the examples of course goals and objectives in Chapters 3 and 4.

Step Two: Prepare the Assessment Instrument

There are many different kinds of assessment instruments you can use in law school. Illustration 7-2 includes some of these.

Illustration 7-2. Assessment Instruments

1. Multiple-choice and short answer quizzes
2. Analytical, issue-spotting, and advocacy essays
3. Outlines, charts and matrices
4. Legal documents such as wills, articles of incorporation, injunctions, statutes
5. Journals
6. Role-plays—simulations with students engaged in practice-related performances
7. Verbal presentations and oral arguments
8. Skits, movies, games, artwork, … and on and on.

Regardless of the kind of assessment you are doing, as you prepare the instrument, consider the factors described below and listed in Illustration 7-3.

Illustration 7-3. Factors to Consider When Preparing Assessment Instruments

- What is the rationale for this assessment?
- What do you want students to do?
- What is the assessment's content?
- How will you provide feedback?

By providing answers to these questions, you can prevent a lot of wasted time and effort—yours and the students'.

Provide the Rationale for the Assessment

Make sure your students know *why* you are asking them to perform the assessment and what feedback they can expect. For example:

> *Let's figure out how this rule applies. I'm giving you some facts and am asking you to make a decision. After you make your decisions, we'll discuss some valid responses. This interaction will give you practice and verbal feedback on applying this rule.*

Be Explicit about What Students Should Do

Provide ultra-precise and clear directions. Give students plenty of white space, use bullets, numbers, and different forms of emphasis to help them stay on task. Write all directions in plain English, using sentences of 25 words or less and paragraphs of 4–8 sentences. Unless you intend an ambiguity, there should no doubt about what students are expected to do.

If possible, give students the directions before a graded assessment. It can reduce needless stress if students know what they will be expected to do and are aware of the exam's format, number of questions and time allotted.

Ask specific questions, such as, "Is this a valid trust? Why or why not?" rather than "Discuss plaintiff's claims." Similarly, when presenting a hypothetical problem, be clear about whether students should be selective about what facts they apply or identify as many as possible. In addition consider telling students what *not* do. For example: "Please focus on the problematic aspects of the articles of incorporation. **Do not** discuss the provisions that are clear. **If at all possible, do the assessment yourself, revising it based on what you want to emphasize.**

Tell students how much time they have to complete the assessment. Students will usually take twice as much time as you would to complete an assessment. If you don't have the time to do the assessment yourself, see how long it takes to prepare your outline.

Ask a colleague to track how long it took just to read the assessment. Provide sufficient time in or out of class to allow well-prepared students to complete the assessment. If the graded assessment has time constraints, suggest amounts of time for each section as students have a hard time budgeting their time.

Direct students about any particular format or approach they should use, especially if the assessment is graded. How many minutes should their presentations be? Can they use props in their simulations? Should they dress up? Are they expected to speak loudly enough to be heard at the back of the room? Do you have preferences about margins, font type and size, page length, spacing and organizational structure? Alternatively, you may want to leave the options wide open to allow for a greater range of student creativity.

To maximize the benefits of collaboration, some assessments can be group projects, and some a hybrid, such as asking students to prepare an assessment individually and then collaborate with others who have similarly prepared. Another possibility is to have students take an assessment individually but to award a bonus to all the members of a group if everyone in the group performs at or above a predetermined level, such as 80% correct.

Determine the Content of the Assessment

Keeping your learning goals in mind, focus assessments on the most important skills, content, and values in the course. During the course, give students practice integrating different areas by embedding material from an earlier section of the course in a new assessment.

Designing fact patterns or hypotheticals. Consult casebooks, court opinions, restatements, journals, and current events for ideas about realistic scenarios.

Omit distractions that could impede students' learning. For example, using a rape scenario on a criminal exam may provoke powerfully negative emotional responses in students who have been sexually assaulted. Avoid using unexplained references or making assumptions about students' cultural experiences or background knowledge. For example, omit sports references or names of TV shows that may be meaningless to some students.

Keep names simple. Give every person in an assessment a different sounding name. Using one-syllable names that start with "P" or "D" makes it clear who the plaintiffs and defendants are. Include realistic names of corporations, towns, and statutes, such as "Chemical Co." rather than "Big Bad Corp."

Consider including a visual. A photo, a map or other visual can help students more quickly understand the scenario you want them to analyze.

Avoid humor on graded assessments; students do not find graded assessments funny.

Determine How You Will Provide Students with Feedback

You could give "global feedback" where you review all assessments and then provide comments on common themes. You can select excerpts from a few sample assessments and comment on the common strengths and weaknesses. You can also provide a sample answer that students can compare with their written submissions. Students could review and comment upon their peers' work. You can provide a checklist or rubric students can use to self-assess. (More on rubrics below). If you're new at providing feedback, you may want to tell students that you will provide feedback and will determine the particular method after you've seen their work.

Step Three: Give Feedback to Students

The most effective feedback is:

1. **Specific** — information about specific criteria students have or have not met.
2. **Positive** — students find out what they are doing well.
3. **Corrective** — students learn about their weaknesses and get strategies to improve them.

4. **Prompt**—students get feedback while the assessment is
    fresh and before the next one.

Provide Students with Specific Feedback

Focus on one to three key components that could be improved.
One way to give feedback is to first take the assessment yourself,
analyze your response, and then make a list of specific things you
wanted students to show on this assessment. Use the list to work
through student assessments, putting a "check," "check plus," or
"check minus" on their work and returning them to students in the
next class.

You also can give specific feedback verbally in class, such as by
saying,

> *"Excellent! Jana named some critical facts in applying this
> rule. Each fact helps show why the plaintiff lost. In prac-
> tice it's essential to show **how** the facts apply to the law."*

Another way to provide specific feedback is to give students a
rubric—a grid with a set of detailed written criteria used to assess
student performance. Illustration 7-4 shows a sample rubric from
a criminal procedure course. Students and teachers can assess performance more effectively when they have a rubric describing specific criteria and levels of quality.

Provide Students with Positive Feedback

Most students learn more effectively when they are validated for
what they do well. Give positive feedback at the beginning, even if
all you can say is "Nice job using the accurate regulation" to help
them build on their successes.

Give Students Feedback about Their Weaknesses and Provide Strategies to Improve Them

- Be direct but compassionate;
- Sandwich specific corrective feedback in between positive
  feedback;

Illustration 7-4. Sample Rubric

The categories to the right do not necessarily correlate with end of semester grades. → Description of what is being assessed ↓	Levels of quality		
	Exemplary	**Competent**	**Developing**
Identifies basic and complex criminal procedural issues — "Issue Spotting" 40%	❏ Accurately identifies *all* basic procedural issues *21–30 points* ❏ Identifies *most* of the complex issues *7–10 points*	❏ Accurately identifies *most* basic procedural issues *11–20 points* ❏ Identifies *some* of the more complex issues *4–6 points*	❏ Accurately identifies *some* basic procedural issues *0–10 points* ❏ Identifies a *few* of the more complex issues *0–3 points*
Analyzes the facts 40%	❏ Accurately and explicitly shows how the law applies to important facts *27–40 points*	❏ Accurately shows how the law applies to most of the relevant facts *14–26 points*	❏ Accurately but minimally shows how the law applies to some of the facts *0–13 points*
Identifies and applies the policy for the rules of criminal procedure 20%	❏ Identifies and applies competing policy goals to facts in predicting results *14–20 points*	❏ Somewhat identifies and applies policy to facts in predicting results *7–13 points*	❏ Minimally identifies and applies policy to facts in predicting results *0–6 points*

- Focus on the work, not the person;
- Avoid making normative judgments; and
- Provide strategies to improve.

Examples: *"Your mock client interview would have been more effective if you had stated your advice in simpler language."*

"Great mistake! This document includes exactly what was asked for—factual inferences. Now consider which inferences are reasonable; how might you explain them to a lay person?"

Avoid Making Assumptions

You may assume a student's poor performance shows a lack of effort. Instead, the student may have been facing a crisis or need additional coaching. It also is possible your directions were unclear. But do tell students when their work suggests that they may fail the course. It's a hard message to deliver and to hear, but the message will be even more painful if the student earns the D or F.

Give Students Prompt Feedback

The shorter the assessment, and the fewer the students, the sooner students should receive feedback. Give feedback on a short in-class quiz or hypothetical during that class or the next. For longer or more complex assessments, give feedback within one or two weeks. Leverage your resources by enlisting others to help — invite other teachers and lawyers to provide feedback as well as asking your students to read and comment upon each other's work or their own work, comparing assessments with samples, checklists, or rubrics that you provide. Giving feedback is crucial to our students' success in law school and in practice. Start small, use a variety of feedback methods, and continue to reflect on what works, as suggested in Chapter 8.

Using Classroom Assessment Techniques to Improve Your Teaching

Classroom assessments help you see what students **are actually learning** during the class, allowing you to revise your teaching based on what you learn. One of our favorites is the **Minute Paper**. At any point in a class session, identify a discreet question or prompt to which you want students to respond. Put the question/prompt on the board, slide, or a quarter or half sheet of paper. Ask students to take a minute to respond. Here are a few examples of the kinds of questions that can work well:

- "Identify a major factor in determining the 'best interests of the child.'"
- "What was the muddiest point of today's discussion?"
- "How confident are you about your ability to learn environmental law?"

Collect and scan through responses. Note general themes and give feedback in the next class, "Almost everyone had a question about federal preemption. Let me try to clarify ..."

Evaluating Students to Assign Grades— The Hardest Part of Assessment

For grades to have integrity, graded assessments must be valid and reliable. Students should only earn a grade after having multiple and varied assessments which are fairly administered (see Illustration 7-5.)

Illustration 7-5. Evaluating Students to Assign Grades— Essential Elements

1. Use multiple assessments
2. Use a variety of assessments
3. Evaluate fairly:
   - Test what you teach—provide students with grading criteria in advance
   - Give students time to practice meeting criteria before they are graded
   - Use explicit criteria to ensure consistent grading
   - Show students how they met grading criteria—make the grading process also a learning process

Essential Elements

Use Multiple Assessments

Any of the assessments from Illustration 7-2 can contribute to students' grades. Example:

- 15% for class contributions (professional engagement in and outside of class);
- 25% for a midterm exam (half essay and half multiple-choice questions); and
- 60% on the final exam (essay and multiple-choice questions).

Use a Variety of Assessments

Because the practice of law is multi-dimensional and because students can demonstrate competency in many ways, use a range of graded assessments. See Illustration 7-2 for ideas.

Evaluate Fairly

Test what you teach and provide students with grading criteria in advance. Identify what you want students to learn by the end of the course, and check that your class sessions work towards those goals. As you construct your assessment instruments, review the goals to ensure that you test students on those goals. Provide students with a list of criteria or a rubric, such as the rubric in Illustration 7-3, to help them focus on those criteria and develop independent learning skills. If you are using oral presentations as an evaluative assessment, you could similarly describe the grading criteria and relative weights:

- Content—clear, organized and coherent—50%
- Visual aids—handouts, slides, props used to enhance content—20%
- Delivery—audible, clear, varied, responsive and within time limits—10%
- Creativity—shows innovation in presenting and engaging classmates—20%

By articulating the criteria in writing, we name what we mean by "analyze the following problem." Usually, we learn that we are expecting far more from students than we realized. Naming the criteria also keeps students from wasting energy trying to figure out what we want.

Give students time to practice meeting criteria before they are graded. It's only fair to allow students to practice and get feedback on exams, quizzes, drafts, or mock performances before they have to take assessments for a grade.

Use explicit criteria to ensure consistent grading. When teachers have explicit criteria, such as checklists or rubrics, they grade consistently and reliably, and maintain high expectations. They are also more efficient in the long term. Creating a rubric takes time but the early investment pays off during the actual grading.

Show students how they met grading criteria—make the grading process a learning process. If the graded assessment occurs before the end of the semester, hold a review session to go over the assessment or spend time in class reviewing it. Allow students to see or have the checklists or rubrics you used to assign their grades. Ask several students who have done well for permission to use their work as examples. Let students learn what good work can look like. If you want to reuse part of an assessment, allow students to review their exams and feedback material over a few weeks, taking notes, but not making copies.

If students want to meet with you to go over a grade, do the following.

- *Use the 24-hour rule.* Talk to students after they have had their graded assessment for 24 hours; this practice gives everyone a little breathing space.
- *Ask to meet with the student in person.* Meeting in person ensures a more productive conversation. We find email usually very ineffective.
- *Require students to review all materials and prepare questions before meeting with you individually.* This requirement makes the experience much more manageable and specific. If students

challenge the grade, ask them to show you where they met the criteria in their assessment.

- *Almost never change a grade; if you do, only do it slowly and very carefully.* Follow your institution's rules about grade changes. If you learn of a mathematical error, review that exam and score sheet and cause of the mistake. If the error is in more than one place, consider how you can fix the problem across the class.
- *Limit the time in which students can talk to you about a graded assessment.* Once grades are out, give students two to four weeks to contact you with questions.

The Grading Process Itself — Designing and Using Rubrics/Scoring Sheets — One Way

As used below, the term "exam" means any graded assessment.

- Jump right in. Delaying the process makes it harder and more stressful.
- Figure out how much time you have until you must submit grades to the registrar.
- Skim seven to ten exams, developing checklists about effective responses.
- Draft the rubric, setting the weights of different components — is spotting tricky issues more important than spotting basic issues?
- Use the draft rubric to score ten exams. Set aside these first ten exams; track their numbers.
- Keeping a list, spreadsheet, or other method to track exam numbers, continue using rubrics to score exams. Revise the rubric as necessary — students always surprise us. (Have a "bonus" category for material that otherwise demonstrates attainment of course goals.)

- If the exam has more than one part, such as three essays, grade all students' Essay #1s only. When you have scored all Essay #1s, grade the Essay #2s. This approach helps reduce "drift," where performance on one part of an exam influences another part of that exam.
- Vary the order in which you grade. If you graded the first essays starting with low numbers, grade the second essays starting with the middle or highest numbers.
- Use a pencil or have white-out handy.
- Take breaks every hour, even if you don't think you need it. You'll be more efficient in the long run.
- When you have finished grading, revisit the first ten you graded. If you notice significant discrepancies from later ones, revise and continue to review until you find that the scores you gave earlier are consistent. Remember, a detailed scoring sheet will make you far more consistent.
- Total scores. You may want to review the handful of highest and lowest scores.
- Look for trends in scores. Capture that information with your course notes (see Chapter 8) for the next time you teach the course.
- Submit grades.
- Once you have submitted your grades, identify a few students who earned high scores on different parts of the exam. Request their permission for you to use their unidentified answers as samples of high quality student work.
- Take notes for yourself about grading to help you the next time.

Checklist for Assessing Student Learning

Illustration 7-6 is a checklist you can use as you work through the assessment process.

Illustration 7-6. Assessing Student Learning Checklist

Using assessment to improve student learning and your teaching

❏ **Identify discreet learning objectives** — the knowledge, skills and values you want students learn in your course.

❏ **Prepare and give assessment instruments**
  ❏ Identify the reason you are giving the assessment
  ❏ Be explicit about what you want students to do
  ❏ What is the assessment's content?
  ❏ How will you provide feedback?

❏ **Give feedback to students**
  ❏ **Specific.** Students get information about specific criteria.
  ❏ **Positive.** Students find out what they are doing well.
  ❏ **Corrective.** Students learn about their weaknesses and strategies to improve them.
  ❏ **Prompt.** Students get feedback while the assessment is fresh.

Evaluating students to assign grades

❏ Use multiple assessments
❏ Use a variety of assessments
❏ **Evaluate fairly:**
  ❏ Test what you teach — provide students with grading criteria in advance
  ❏ Give students time to practice meeting criteria before they are graded
  ❏ Use explicit criteria to ensure consistent grading
  ❏ Show students how they met grading criteria — make the grading process also a learning process

Engage in ongoing assessment

You will find examples of the concepts from this chapter in Appendix 7 on the book's website — http://lawteaching.org/resources/books/teachinglawbydesign/teachinglawbydesign-appendices.pdf.

Appendix 7-1: Assessment Instruments
        Peer Feedback Formative Assessment Exercise
        Midterm/Peer Feedback, Reflection Assessment
        Guidelines for Phase III: Reflection
        International Environmental Law Quiz
        Civil Procedure — Reflections on Civil Litigation

Appendix 7-2: Rubrics
        Torts Rubric
        Rubric/Scoring Sheet
        Remedies Peer Review Rubric
        Client Letter Rubric
        Clinical Rubric-Performance Competencies

Chapter 8

Developing as a Teacher

The central aim of this book is to produce significant student learning by designing, delivering, and assessing law school courses and classes. An underlying premise is that teachers play a meaningful role in students' learning. The focus of this chapter is on your continued professional development as teachers. How can you enhance your students' learning by continuing to improve your teaching?

Sustaining a Teaching Practice

Nearly all adjunct professors are motivated primarily by the intrinsic rewards of teaching. This intrinsic motivation spurs adjuncts to seek feedback on their performance and new strategies to improve their teaching.

Although continued professional development as teachers can provide great satisfaction and reward, we should acknowledge the obstacles that hinder growth. Faculty misconceptions about teaching and learning present obstacles. Misconceptions include (1) if you know the content well, you can teach well; (2) you should master one teaching technique that suits your style and stick with it; and (3) good teachers are born, not made. Research debunks all of these myths: (1) effective teaching requires knowledge of content coupled with pedagogical skill; (2) no single teaching method works for every student or accomplishes every educational goal; and (3) successful teachers learn how to teach and continue to improve their skills throughout their careers. Further, continuing to develop teaching skills, a complex, human activity, is not easy. As we learn more about teaching and learning, we may uncover shortcomings in our current philosophy and practice. It is common for us to struggle as we try new methods. Sustained development in teaching requires hard work and perseverance.

The challenges and rewards of ongoing efforts to improve teaching apply to all faculty, not just new teachers or those who are struggling in the classroom. All of us can enhance our effectiveness through reflection, feedback, and innovation.

Most models of teaching development involve several stages: instructional awareness, formative feedback, pedagogical knowledge, implementation, and assessment.

- **Instructional awareness.** The first step in the process of improving instruction is to increase our understanding of our own teaching philosophy and practices. What do we believe are the purposes of legal education and our roles as teachers? What assumptions do we make about teaching and learning? What behaviors do we exhibit when we interact with students in and out of the classroom? Are our teaching methods consistent with our educational philosophy?
- **Formative feedback.** Formative feedback is critical to improving teaching and learning. To make effective changes in teaching, we need to know the strengths and weaknesses of our current practices and their effect on students' learning. We can gather that information from ourselves, students, colleagues, and consultants.
- **Pedagogical knowledge.** Deeper understanding of student learning and teaching methods can help us put the feedback we receive in context. We can gain valuable insights from scholarship about learning theory, student motivation, and learning styles. Likewise, the literature on teaching methods, instructional design, educational technology, and assessment inform our choices about appropriate adjustments in our teaching.
- **Implementation.** Teaching improvement occurs through changes in our teaching philosophy, attitudes, and behavior. Numerous resources are available to assist us at this stage —

books, articles, websites, and videotapes on teaching; discussions with colleagues; working with consultants. To be effective, these changes should be incremental and systematic. A good start in teaching improvement could entail one or two small changes implemented throughout a course.

- **Assessment.** The final stage is for us to evaluate the effectiveness of our teaching improvement efforts. Did our changes in philosophy, attitudes, and practices improve our teaching and our students' learning? This information forms the basis for the next cycle in our teaching development.

Many types of faculty development activities are available for teachers who want to increase their effectiveness. In 2006, we surveyed law teachers throughout the United States regarding their participation in activities to improve teaching. These teaching improvement activities are discussed below. Many of these take some time but are very low cost.

Self-Assessment, Reflection, and Study

Many faculty members provide their own faculty development through individual assessment, reflection, and study. For many of us, the most important source of information is our own observations and reflection on our teaching.

Benefits of Reflective Practice

Self-study and reflection can help us to become more aware of our teaching assumptions and behaviors, to articulate a coherent teaching rationale, and to make informed changes in our instructional practices. Most teachers have deeply ingrained assumptions about teaching and learning, which affect teaching behavior. To grow as teachers, we must identify our current assumptions and behavior that may be hindering our effectiveness. Our observations and reflection can reveal patterns of behavior, habitual responses, underlying motivations, and aspects of our teaching that need improvement. Reflective teachers are able to explain the rationale behind their teaching. That rationale can give us confidence and serve as the foundation for our teaching choices. As a result of examining assumptions and developing a rationale, reflective teachers modify their plans, attitudes, and actions in the classroom.

These benefits of reflective practice are supported by empirical research. Our survey respondents concluded that reflection on their teaching before and after class is effective in increasing their awareness of their teaching philosophy and practices, improving their level of confidence, and increasing their enthusiasm and passion for teaching. Further, law teachers rated reflection (thinking about teaching and keeping a journal about teaching) as the faculty development activities most effective in producing changes in their teaching practices.

Self-Assessment

Evaluation forms and inventories can help teachers engage in self-assessment. We can analyze our teaching behaviors by completing the same course evaluation form that the students fill out at the end of the term. The results can be revealing. Most teachers' self-assessments of their strengths and weaknesses agree with their students' assessments.

Inventories help teachers assess the presence, absence, and extent of instructional behaviors. Inventories adapted to legal education allow us assess our teaching in the context of seven empirically derived principles for enhancing learning: Encouraging student-faculty contact; fostering cooperation among students; encouraging active learning, giving prompt feedback; emphasizing time on task; communicating high expectations; and respecting diverse talents and ways of learning. All seven inventories are accessible on the book's website.

Teaching Journal

An excellent tool for reflection is a teaching journal. The process of keeping a professional journal promotes reflection. Journals are a useful device for creating a comprehensive account of our experience. The journal is a place to record problems, successes, strategies for improvement, and ideas for subsequent classes. Because journal entries are made close in time to our experiences, they are often more accurate than our recollections months after the events. Journal writing helps us to clarify our assumptions and theories about teaching and learning, to evaluate the effectiveness of instructional practices, and to identify alternative methods to try in the future. Further, teaching journals are tools for setting goals, planning individual class sessions, and restructuring courses. We can use journals to analyze problems and to work through the strong emotions that accompany teaching. Finally, journal writing can be a vehicle for us to integrate our personal and professional selves and to engage in a lifelong, reflective learning process.

Law teachers who keep a teaching journal rated it as the single most effective faculty development device for prompting actual changes in teaching behavior. Yet, only 9% of the respondents to our survey keep a teaching journal. Why? Keeping a teaching journal is not easy. It takes time, energy, and discipline. And journal writing does not fit the learning style of every teacher; some of us are more comfortable talking about our experiences than writing about them.

Several practical aspects of the journal writing process can make it more fun and valuable:

- Space. Find a comfortable place to write free of distractions—in the office with the door closed, in a coffee shop, or at home in a comfortable chair.
- Time. Schedule time for journal writing; for example, twice a week for thirty minutes or after each class for ten minutes.
- Format. There are many options to fit individual preferences—bound journal books, three ring binders, an artist's sketchbook, a computer.

- Commitment. Put journal time on the calendar and treat it like a professional appointment.
- Trust the process. Don't censor. Insight and progress can follow paragraphs of bland, uninspired writing.
- Content. Free-writing in which we describe and explore our experiences is a common form of journaling. An alternative is to write in response to a prompt. You can find reflection prompts on the book's website.

Print and Electronic Resources

Numerous print and electronic resources facilitate self-directed faculty development. Journal articles, books, newsletters, videotapes, and websites address the theory and practice of teaching and learning. Law teachers regularly engage in this type of development — over 80% of our survey respondents reported reading journal articles on teaching and learning and 33% read books on those topics. Using these resources can help us improve our teaching in several ways — by causing us to reflect on our instructional practices, by giving us ideas, and by inspiring us to take reasonable risks and exert the effort needed to improve teaching and learning. Chapter 9 provides a gateway to the teaching and learning literature.

Formative Feedback from Students

Feedback from students about our teaching and their learning is an important part of faculty development. Over 90% of our survey respondents review student evaluations after the course. In addition, about 50% of the respondents gather feedback from students about teaching effectiveness during the course.

Student Evaluations

Extensive empirical research in higher education demonstrates the value of student evaluations for faculty development. Dozens of studies reveal a persistent positive effect of written feedback from students on subsequent teaching effectiveness. Written student comments provide us with formative feedback and helpful suggestions regarding our clarity, delivery, organization, punctuality, fairness, demeanor, and availability outside of class.

Despite the potential benefits of end-of-the-term student evaluations for faculty development, some law teachers are reluctant to use them for development purposes. Their reluctance may come from a lack of confidence in the value of student evaluations and the pain that comes from reviewing negative comments. The following ideas may help maximize the usefulness of student evaluations and minimize the discomfort from negative comments.

- Look at the numerical evaluations and read quickly though the comments to get an overall sense of the students' reaction to the course. The first time though the evaluations, many teachers focus on the lower scores and negative comments.
- Review the numerical evaluations a second time to analyze the results. Compare the scores on each item to scores from the previous time or two that you taught the course. Pay attention to the trend in the scores.
- Review the comments a second time to identify themes. Articulate in writing several categories of positive comments. Identify in writing one or two areas in which the students made negative comments or suggested improvement. Compare the positive and negative themes to comments in previous student evaluations.
- Choose an area or two to address the next time you teach the course. Make incremental, not wholesale, changes.
- Try to ignore isolated mean comments, such as "I learned nothing in this course" or "Professor X should be fired." These

types of comments are a reflection on the commentator's problems, not our teaching.

- Have a colleague or consultant review your student evaluations. Another set of eyes can help us see the positive aspects of the evaluations and can assist us in identifying trends, themes, and appropriate adjustments to make in the future.

Feedback from Students during the Course

Gathering formative feedback from students during the course helps us improve our teaching. Our survey respondents rated "gathering and reviewing feedback from students about own teaching during a course" as an effective means of improving teaching in three ways: improving their level of confidence in their teaching, increasing their enthusiasm and passion for teaching, and making changes in teaching practices. The classroom assessment methods described in Chapter 7 help teachers gather feedback from students about their learning and make reasonable adjustments in teaching methods during the rest of the course to maximize students' learning.

Teachers can design short written questionnaires to obtain detailed feedback from students during the course to improve teaching. The questionnaire can focus on a specific aspect of teaching or the course as a whole. For example, the questionnaire could ask three questions: (1) What teaching/learning methods have been *most* effective for you in this course? (2) What teaching/learning methods have been *least* effective for you in this course? (3) What other teaching/learning methods should we try in this course?

Keep the questionnaire process simple. Design a one-page form with three to five questions. Explain to students the purpose of the questionnaire—to gather feedback to make your teaching and their learning more effective. Distribute the form in class. Have your students respond anonymously. Collect and review the responses, looking for prevalent themes. Within a week, report briefly to the class about the common responses to each of the questions. Inform students of at least one suggestion that you intend to implement.

Teachers who use questionnaires during the course can experience several types of benefits. First, students' responses should provide specific feedback and suggestions to improve teaching and learning. Further, the process of seeking feedback from students and implementing reasonable suggestions shows our deep respect for students. Many students will respond by working hard to achieve the goals of the course. Finally, the questionnaire process demonstrates a critical life-long, professional skill—welcoming and profiting from constructive feedback.

Collaborating with Colleagues

Our colleagues are valuable teaching development resources. Over 90% of our survey respondents talk with colleagues about teaching as one form of faculty development. Around 50% have observed a colleague's classes to provide feedback or had fellow teachers observe their classes for development purposes.

Discussions with Colleagues

Talking with colleagues about teaching and learning is a common and effective type of development activity. In our survey, law teachers rated this activity as effective on every dimension of teaching development:

- Increasing their awareness of their own teaching practice and philosophy;
- Increasing their knowledge of teaching and learning principles;
- Improving their level of confidence in their teaching;
- Increasing their enthusiasm or passion for teaching; and
- Making changes in their teaching practices.

Peer Observations and Feedback

Peer observations can be especially valuable if pairs of colleagues agree to observe one another's classes. The reciprocal nature of the observations creates mutual vulnerability and shared responsibility. The colleagues can follow a three-step process.

First, the colleagues meet for a pre-observation conference. They discuss their approaches to teaching, goals for the course as a whole and class to be observed, material for the class, expectations for student preparation, what students will do during the class, and the teaching methods to be used. Most importantly, they tell one another the specific types of feedback they would like to receive. Areas for feedback could include organization, clarity, use of visual aids, types of questions, handling student responses, teacher's verbal and nonverbal communication, level of student engagement during class, number of women and men speaking in class, etc.

Second, the pairs visit each other's classes and gather the requested feedback. For example, if the teacher requests feedback on questioning, the observer could write out every question the teacher asks during the class; if the teacher wants feedback on student engagement, the observer could note what the students are doing at one-minute intervals during the class.

Third, the colleagues meet for a post-observation conference. Those discussions should include the specific feedback requested in the pre-observation conference, both teachers' positive and negative reactions, the extent to which the goals for the class were accomplished, and an exploration of alternative methods to achieve course objectives.

In addition to classroom visits, colleagues are ideally situated to help one another with course design, materials, and evaluation instruments. Peers can provide formative feedback on syllabi, course web pages, readings and other assignments. Colleagues can be especially helpful in reviewing the materials related to evaluating student work: quizzes and tests (both graded and ungraded) as well as paper and presentation assignments.

Consultants

Teaching development consultants can be national "experts" from outside of the institution, members of a university teaching excellence center, or faculty members from within the law school with expertise in teaching and learning. The roles of consultants and colleagues in faculty development can overlap quite a bit. Consultants or colleagues can conduct classroom observations, review course materials, engage in individual coaching, and work with peers who record their teaching.

Video recording can be a particularly powerful device for assessing and improving our classroom communication skills. A video of a class provides accurate, reliable, audio and visual feedback of several areas of our classroom performance:

- Verbal communication — clarity of speech, volume, verbal ticks
- Visual aids — legibility of board work, visual impact of computer presentations
- Nonverbal behavior — eye contact, movement, gestures
- Questioning — types of questions we ask and how we handle student responses
- Other presentation skills, including organization, flow, pacing, and variety in methods.

Despite the value of video recording in faculty development, many teachers are reluctant to be recorded. Only 17% of our survey respondents report viewing a video of their own teaching. Their reluctance may be due to anxiety about the recording and review, which can reveal communication glitches and dramatically illustrate to teachers the disparity between their self-image and the behavior they see on the video.

Several techniques can minimize the anxiety and maximize the value of video recording and review.

1. Select a "typical" class to be recorded. Explain to students that the purpose of the video is to provide feedback on your teaching, not to record their performance.

2. View the video soon after the class while the class is fresh in your mind. View the recording once to get used to seeing yourself on video and to get over the natural tendency to focus on minor distractions—Do I really sound like that? Look like that? Have those mannerisms?

3. View the video a second time with a supportive colleague who can provide perspective and can help you focus on specific strengths and weaknesses rather than the minor distractions (voice, appearance) that have little to do with effective teaching.

4. Use a checklist to help you assess significant components of teaching, such as organization, visual aids, clarity of presentation, questioning, and student participation.

5. Use the video to generate detailed data on specific aspects of your teaching. For example, record every question you ask and analyze the clarity and depth of each question. Or keep track of what is happening at minute intervals—teacher talk? Student question? Student comment? Exercise?

6. With the assistance of a colleague or consultant, choose one or two aspects of your teaching to address in response to the feedback from your review of the video.

7. Keep control of the video. It is yours. Save it to review in the future and compare to subsequent videos of your teaching. Or destroy it if that makes you more comfortable.

Teaching Workshops and Conferences

Teaching effectiveness workshops rank among the most popular faculty development activities. Approximately half of law teachers responding to our faculty development survey report attending a workshop on pedagogy at their own institution. About one quarter of the respondents attended a national or regional teaching conference, sponsored by Association of American Law Schools, CALI, the Legal Writing Institute, the Society of American Law Teachers, or the Institute for Law Teaching and Learning. Even though your institution may not provide funds for you to travel to a national conference, you may find local or regional conferences that do not charge fees.

Among the twenty-two activities assessed in the faculty development survey, attending a national or regional conference or workshop was among the most effective. Attending these conferences was rated as the most effective in three dimensions: (1) increasing a teacher's knowledge of teaching and learning principles; (2) improving a teacher's confidence in teaching; and (3) increasing a teacher's enthusiasm and passion for teaching. The value of attending national or regional conferences is further supported by a survey that we conducted five years after an AALS teaching and learning conference held in 2001. Most of the respondents reported that their attendance at the conference increased their reflection on teaching methods (97%), knowledge of teaching and learning principles (96%), awareness of their own teaching philosophy (95%), confidence (71%), and enthusiasm for teaching (70%). In addition, 93% of the respondents implemented changes in their teaching practices as a result of the conference.

Checklist for Teaching Development

Illustration 8-1 is a checklist you can use to guide your continued development as a teacher.

Illustration 8-1. Teaching Development Checklist

❏ **Self assessment, reflection, and study**
  ❏ Thinking about effective teaching methods before and after class
  ❏ Reading books and articles on teaching and learning
  ❏ Completing inventories on teaching practices
  ❏ Keeping a teaching journal

❏ **Formative feedback from students**
  ❏ Reviewing student evaluations of your teaching after the course
  ❏ Gathering feedback from students on your teaching during the course

❏ **Collaborating with colleagues**
  ❏ Talking with colleagues about teaching and learning
  ❏ Observing a colleague's class and providing feedback
  ❏ Having a colleague observe your class and provide feedback

❏ **Working with a consultant**
  ❏ Receiving individual coaching on teaching strengths and weaknesses
  ❏ Reviewing video of your teaching

❏ **Teaching workshops and conferences**
  ❏ Attending a national or regional conference on teaching and learning
  ❏ Attending a workshop at your institution on teaching and learning

You will find examples of the concepts from this chapter in Appendix 8 on the book's website — http://lawteaching.org/resources/books/teachinglawbydesign/teachinglawbydesign-appendices.pdf.

Appendix 8-1: Principles for Enhancing Student Learning — Faculty Inventory

Appendix 8-2: Reflection Prompts

Selected Resources — Books, Articles, Newsletters, Videos, and Websites

The print and electronic literature on teaching and learning in higher education and law school is enormous. Excellent resources addressing both theory and practice abound for teachers who want to know more and to improve their skills. Below we have collected the books, articles, newsletters, videotapes, and websites on which we relied in writing this book (along with a few others that we just couldn't resist including). We encourage you to sample these and other resources as you seek to enhance your teaching and your students' learning. And we apologize to the authors of the many wonderful resources that are not listed here.

Books

American Bar Association, Adjunct Faculty Handbook (2005) (available at http://www.abanet.org/legaled/publications/adjunct handbook/adjuncthandbook.pdf).

Thomas A. Angelo & K. Patricia Cross, Classroom Assessment Techniques: A Handbook for College Teachers (2d ed. 1993).

Ken Bain, What the Best College Teachers Do (2004).

Charles C. Bonwell & James E. Eison, Active Learning: Creating Excitement in the Classroom (1991).

JOHN BRANSFORD ET. AL., HOW PEOPLE LEARN: BRAIN, MIND, EX-
     PERIENCE, AND SCHOOL (National Academies Press, 2000) (avail-
     able at http://www.napedu/ books/0309070368/html).
STEPHEN BROOKFIELD, BECOMING A CRITICALLY REFLECTIVE
     TEACHER (1995).
STEPHEN BROOKFIELD, THE SKILLFUL TEACHER (2d ed. 2006).
STEPHEN BROOKFIELD & STEPHEN PRESKILL, DISCUSSION AS A WAY
     OF TEACHING: TOOLS AND TECHNIQUES FOR DEMOCRATIC
     CLASSROOMS (1999).
PATRICIA CRANTON, (ED.) AUTHENTICITY IN TEACHING (2006).
BARBARA GROSS DAVIS, TOOLS FOR TEACHING (1993).
WALTER O. DICK, LOU CAREY & JAMES O. CAREY, THE SYSTEMATIC
     DESIGN OF INSTRUCTION (6th ed. 2005).
L. DEE FINK, CREATING SIGNIFICANT LEARNING EXPERIENCES
     (2003).
DONALD L. FINKEL, TEACHING WITH YOUR MOUTH SHUT (2000).
STEVEN FRIEDLAND & GERALD F. HESS, TEACHING THE LAW SCHOOL
     CURRICULUM (2004).
FRANK HEPPNER, TEACHING THE LARGE COLLEGE CLASS (2007).
GERALD F. HESS & STEVEN FRIEDLAND, TECHNIQUES FOR TEACH-
     ING LAW (1999).
LARRY KEIG & MICHAEL D. WAGGONER, COLLABORATIVE PEER RE-
     VIEW: THE ROLE OF FACULTY IN IMPROVING COLLEGE TEACH-
     ING (1994).
JOSEPH LOWMAN, MASTERING THE TECHNIQUES OF TEACHING (2d
     ed. 1995).
ROBERT MACCRATE, REPORT OF THE TASK FORCE ON LAW SCHOOLS
     AND THE PROFESSION: NARROWING THE GAP, 1992 A.B.A. Sec.
     Legal Educ. & Prof. Dev.
PEGGY L. MAKI, ASSESSING FOR LEARNING: BUILDING A SUSTAIN-
     ABLE COMMITMENT ACROSS THE INSTITUTION (2004).
WILBERT J. MCKEACHIE, TEACHING TIPS: STRATEGIES, RESEARCH
     AND THEORY FOR COLLEGE AND UNIVERSITY TEACHERS (12th
     ed. 2005).
LARRY K. MICHAELSEN, ARLETTA BAUMAN KNIGHT AND L. DEE
     FINK, TEAM-BASED LEARNING (2002).

GREGORY S. MUNRO, OUTCOMES ASSESSMENT FOR LAW SCHOOLS 57 (2000).

LINDA NILSON, TEACHING AT ITS BEST (2d ed. 2003).

MICHAEL B. PAULSEN & KENNETH A FELDMAN, TAKING TEACHING SERIOUSLY: MEETING THE CHALLENGE OF INSTRUCTIONAL IMPROVEMENT (1995).

MICHAEL HUNTER SCHWARTZ, EXPERT LEARNING FOR LAW STUDENTS (2d ed. 2008).

MICHAEL HUNTER SCHWARTZ, SOPHIE SPARROW, AND GERALD HESS, TEACHING LAW BY DESIGN: ENGAGING STUDENTS FROM THE SYLLABUS TO THE FINAL EXAM (2009).

PATRICIA L. SMITH & TILLMAN J. RAGAN, INSTRUCTIONAL DESIGN (3d ed. 2005).

DANNELLE D. STEVENS & ANTIONIA LEVI, INTRODUCTION TO RUBRICS (2005).

ROY STUCKEY ET AL., BEST PRACTICES IN LEGAL EDUCATION (2007).

WILLIAM M. SULLIVAN ET AL., EDUCATING LAWYERS: PREPARATION FOR THE PROFESSION OF LAW (2007).

LINDA SUSKIE, ASSESSING STUDENT LEARNING (2004).

BARBARA E. WALVROOD, ASSESSMEMT CLEAR AND SIMPLE: A PRACTICAL GUIDE FOR INSTITUTIONS, DEPARTMENTS, AND GENERAL EDUCATION (2004).

BARBARA E. WALVROOD & VIRGINIA JOHNSON ANDERSON, EFFECTIVE GRADING: A TOOL FOR LEARNING AND ASSESSMENT (1998).

MARYELLEN WEIMER, IMPROVING COLLEGE TEACHING (1990).

MARYELLEN WEIMER, IMPROVING YOUR CLASSROOM TEACHING (1993).

MARYELLEN WEIMER, LEARNER-CENTERED TEACHING: FIVE KEY CHANGES TO PRACTICE (2002).

Articles

Susan B. Apel et. al., *Seven Principles for Good Practice in Legal Education*, 49 J. LEGAL EDUC. 367 (1999) (eight articles applying the seven principles to legal education).

Gerald F. Hess, *Collaborative Course Design: Not My Course, Not Their Course, But Our Course*, 47 WASHBURN L. REVIEW 367 (2007).

Gerald F. Hess, *Heads and Hearts: The Teaching and Learning Environment in Law School*, 52 J. Legal Educ. 75 (2002).

Gerald F. Hess, *Improving Teaching and Learning in Law School: Faculty Development Research, Principles, and Programs*, 12 WIDENER L. REV. 443 (2006).

Gerald F. Hess, *Learning to Think Like a Teacher: Reflective Journals for Legal Educators*, 38 GONZAGA L. REV. 129 (2003).

Gerald F. Hess, *Listening to Our Students: Obstructing and Enhancing Learning in Law School*, 31 U.S.F. L.Rev. 941 (1997).

Gerald F. Hess, *Student Involvement in Improving Law Teaching and Learning*, 67 U.M.K.C. L. REV. 443 (2006).

Gerald F. Hess & Sophie M. Sparrow, *What Helps Law Professors Develop as Teachers?—An Empirical Study*, 14 WIDENER L. REV. 149 (2008).

James B. Levy, *As a Last Resort, Ask the Students: What They say Makes Someone an Effective Law Teacher*, 58 ME. L. REV. 49 (2006).

Michael Hunter Schwartz, *Teaching Law Students to be Self-Regulated Learners*, 2003 MICH. STATE L. REV. 447 (2003).

Michael Hunter Schwartz, *Teaching Law by Design: How Learning Theory and Instructional Design Can Inform and Reform Law Teaching*, 38 SAN DIEGO L. REV. 347 (2001).

Sophie Sparrow, *Describing the Ball: Describing the Ball: Improve Teaching by Using Rubrics—Explicit Grading* Criteria, 2004 MICH. ST. L. REV. 1.

Sophie Sparrow, *Practicing Civility in the Legal Writing Course: Helping Law Students Learn Professionalism*, 13 J. LEG. WRITING 113 (2007).

Kent D. Syverud, *Taking Students Seriously: A Guide for New Law Teachers*, 43 J. Legal Educ. 247 (1993).

Newsletters

The National Teaching & Learning Forum, James Rhem, Executive Editor; 2203 Regent Street, Madison, WI 53726, jrhem@chorus.net; www.ntlf.com.

The Law Teacher, Institute for Law Teaching and Learning, Gerald Hess and Michael Hunter Schwartz, Editors, Gonzaga University School of Law and Washburn University School of Law, http://lawteaching.org.

The Teaching Professor; Maryellen Weimer, Editor; Pennsylvania State University-Berks Campus, P.O. Box 7009, Reading, PA 19610-7009, grg@psu.edu.

Tomorrow's-Professor Mailing List: desk-top faculty development one hundred times a year. Email: Majordomo@lists.standford.edu. Subject: leave blank. Body of message: subscribe tomorrows-professor.

Videos (available at http://lawteaching.org)

Gerald F. Hess, Paula Lustbader, Laurie Zimet, PRINCIPLES TO ENHANCE LEGAL EDUCATION (Inst. for L. Sch. Teaching 2001).

Gerald F. Hess, Paula Lustbader, Laurie Zimet, TEACH TO THE WHOLE CLASS: BARRIERS AND PATHWAYS TO LEARNING (Inst. for L. Sch. Teaching 1997).

Larry Dubin, A DAY IN THE LIFE OF LAW SCHOOL TEACHING, (Inst. For L. Sch. Teaching 1994).

Websites

http://lssse.iub.edu/index.cfm The Law School Survey of Student Engagement is co-sponsored by the American Association of Law Schools (AALS) and the Carnegie Foundation for the Advancement of Teaching and directed by the Indiana School of Education. The Annual Reports for 2003–2007 summarize the survey results for thousands of students at dozens of law schools.

http://bestpracticeslegaled.albanylawblogs.org This blog contains postings on legal education curriculum, teaching, reform, and assessment, providing a web-based source of information on current reforms in legal education arising from the publication of Roy Stuckey's Best Practices for Legal Education and the Carnegie Foundation's Educating Lawyers.

http://idd.elon.edu/blogs/law/ is a blog hosted by Professor Steven Friedland of the Center for Engaged Learning at Elon School of Law. The blog is intended to contribute to the discourse on teaching and learning in law, from the inspirational to the whimsical, to the mechanical. It includes the varying perspectives of teachers, administrators, learners, and practitioners.

http://lawteaching.org The Institute for Law Teaching and Learning serves as a clearinghouse for ideas to improve the quality of education in law school. It publishes an on-line newsletter and its website contains books, articles, videos, and links to law school and higher education. All appendices for *Teaching Law by Design* and *Teaching Law by Design for Adjuncts* are on the ILTL website at http://lawteaching.org/resources/books/teaching lawbydesign/teachinglawbydesign-appendices.pdf.

www.law.umkc.edu/faculty/profiles/glesnerfines/bgf-edu.htm is Professor Barbara Glesner Fines' "Teaching and Learning Law" website which contains helpful materials for law students and teachers.

http://www.washlaw.edu/ This site contains links to over 100 topical sites. The sites — ranging from law schools, to legal books, women in the law, and even every state in the union — are alphabetically organized. The Study Law link, for example, connects the user to links concerning outlines, study aides, other resource guides, and examinations. The Teaching Methods link, on the other hand, connects the user to Web site addresses enabling law school professors to subscribe to educational periodicals.

About the Context and Practice Series

The principles recommended in *Teaching Law By Design for Adjuncts* (and in the larger book, *Teaching Law by Design*, 2009) are embodied in Carolina Academic Press's new Context and Practice Casebook Series. Edited by Michael Hunter Schwartz in consultation with Gerry Hess, the Context and Practice texts are designed based on modern educational theory and provide law teachers with the materials they need to better prepare their students not just to think like lawyers, but to practice like them. In other words, the books strive to implement the recommendations in *Best Practices for Legal Education* and the Carnegie Foundation's *Educating Lawyers: Preparation for the Profession of Law.*

Accordingly, the books in these series offer many improvements to traditional law texts. Books in the Context and Practice Series provide authentic, law practice problems, materials (such as pleadings, contracts, and police reports) and instructional resources designed to contextualize students' doctrinal learning and help students build lawyering skills; include questions and problems that prompt readers to question, reflect, and analyze as they read; engage students in developing their professional identities; guide students' development of self-directed learning strategies; and include teachers' manuals that make it easy to use multiple methods of instruction, to implement meaningful assessment practices without killing oneself, and to emphasize active learning.

For more information on series, go to http://www.cap-press.com/p/CAP. For a listing of available and forthcoming titles, click on the flier link at the bottom of the page.